LEADER'S GUIDE FOR

MIRACLES OF HEALING IN THE GOSPEL OF MARK

John I. Penn Sr.

WESTBOW
PRESS®
A DIVISION OF THOMAS NELSON
& ZONDERVAN

WestBow Press books may be ordered through booksellers or by contacting:

WestBow Press
A Division of Thomas Nelson & Zondervan
1663 Liberty Drive
Bloomington, IN 47403
www.westbowpress.com
844-714-3454

ISBN: 978-1-6642-5312-4 (sc)
ISBN: 978-1-6642-5311-7 (e)

Print information available on the last page.

WestBow Press rev. date: 12/17/2021

Contents

Foreword

T here is no doubt that the ministry of Jesus Christ included preaching, teaching and healing. The Gospels are filled with accounts of Jesus proclaiming that the Kingdom of God had come, teaching people how to live as citizens of this Kingdom (see the "Sermon. On the Mount") and demonstrating the nature and power of God through miracles of healing and casting out demons.

Historically, the majority of churches in the 19th and 20th centuries were comfortable with the preaching and teaching ministry of Jesus. However, Christians who talked about ministry of physical and spiritual healing, or spiritual forces of darkness, or exorcism were considered to be out of touch with modern medicine, science and psychology. Prayers and practices related to the supernatural were replaced by pills, therapy and psychiatric institutions. This was not true for all Christian pastors and institutions— but many. Modernism took over much of the Christian consciousness in North America and Europe.

Now, in the 21st century, we are in a "post-modern" and "post-Christian" context. Relativism and individualism now dominate the world view of North America and Europe. Western popular culture is filled with books and movies about wizards like Harry Potter, zombies that roam the earth, or fictional lands at war with one another. At the same time, growing numbers of young adults identify themselves as "spiritual but not religious," practice yoga and meditation, and have a greater openness to mystery, magic, and paranormal experiences.

Immediately after the terrorist attacks of September 11, 2001, the churches were filled with Americans coming to pray. Within a few weeks, after no additional attacks, the fear of terror faded and church attendance in the USA returned to "normal" and has slowly declined from that day to the present. Today, the trend to abandon the Christian faith of parents and grandparents continues. Why? On the one hand power to heal and transform is rarely seen and celebrated—on the other hand, the call to follow Jesus and engage in his ministry has too many demands on the time and money of busy consumers actively engaged in the search for their own happiness.

The question today is this, "Do the followers of Jesus have the same power to bring healing and transformation life today? Is there a difference between the kingdom of God and the kingdom of the economically privileged world?"

In *Miracles of Healing in the Gospel of Mark* and in this leader's guide, John Penn, clearly answers this question. Like the original book, this leader's guide is clear, theologically substantive, and spiritually rich with insight and invitation. Group leaders will find valuable insights to guide the sessions and significant questions to help everyone to engage the content of each chapter. The author clearly says that there is no single right answer—that is not the goal. The goal of this book is to guide the group experience with humility and substance, offering participants an opportunity to explore their ideas in the context of a prayerful and learning community.

This is a study and leader's guide well worth the time and money. The preaching, teaching and healing ministry of Jesus re-presented to anyone interested in the Christian life today. This resource will help the leader and the group grow spiritually, intellectually, and relationally.

Rev. Thomas R. Albin (Tom)
Executive Director of the United Christian Ashrams International and Former Dean of the Chapel at the Upper Room in Nashville, Tennessee

Introduction

The creation of this *Leader's Guide* will be a welcomed addition to *Miracles of Healing in the Gospel of Mark*. It will provide the resources and tools to equip leaders to help participants have a valuable experience, get the most out of this unique study, and make this resource user-friendly. It will answer the questions included in each of the sixteen Healing Moments and address new and controversial concepts. It will also offer guidance to help the participants stay true to the material's content in each of the Healing Moments. The leader's guide includes a wealth of information and concepts that might be new and challenging.

I want to thank Tom Albin, the Former Dean of the Upper Room Chapel of Nashville, Tennessee, who, several years ago, suggested that I should write a leader's guide for *Miracles of Healing in the Gospel of Mark*. Having taught the book in several Sunday school Bible studies and a Zoom Wednesday Bible study, I strongly agree that this leader's guide will be a Godsend for those using the book to conduct a small group or a church-wide study.

It is essential to know that I did not write *Miracles of Healing in the Gospel of Mark* to provide more information about healing. Mark makes healing central to the kingdom work of God and the church of Jesus Christ. I wrote this resource to help the Christian Church understand why healing was central to Jesus' messianic mission and ministry and the proclamation of the gospel of the kingdom. Secondly,

I also wanted the church to comprehend the biblical, theological, and spiritual connection between healing and salvation.

Healing is not a subject that some churches have felt comfortable introducing to their congregations. We believe that this resource allows the reader to look at the ministry of healing up close and personal, through the eyes, love and the compassionate ministry of Jesus Christ, towards broken humanity. *Miracles of Healing in the Gospel of Mark* can remove the negative concerns that people have toward the ministry of healing.

Healing is a visible sign that God's kingdom has broken into human history. Salvation is to be understood as the ultimate healing. Healing and salvation are the two sides of the same coin. Without this biblical interpretation, healing will always have a secondary role in the life of the church's mission and ministry, which would be contrary to the gospel of Jesus Christ and the kingdom work of God.

The writing of this book has a third and equally important purpose. I want to encourage the reader to realize that God is the same, yesterday, today, and forever. God heals today through the body of Christ, as God healed through Jesus during his earthly mission and ministry (Matt. 10:1-2; Mark 6:12-13; Luke 9:1-2; 10:1-20). God wants human beings to be well and whole. God has empowered the church to be a healing community through the many *charismata*, including the gifts of healing (1Cor. 12:9 NIV). The church has no excuse not to continue Jesus' threefold ministry of teaching, preaching, and healing (John 14:12 NIV).

How to Use This Leader's Guide

We recommend a team approach in using this resource. A team approach will bring a much broader range of skills and experiences to this study. We are not looking for perfect leaders, but leaders committed to biblical integrity and the desire to see the body of Christ become a healing community. The team should spend time praying together and getting to know each other before the study. Prayer should be an intricate part of your preparation and planning to facilitate this study. Planning and preparation should occur at least two months prior to the first session.

Seek the Holy Spirit's guidance to determine how the two of you will share in the responsibilities of this study. Put your plan in writing. Both leaders should keep a copy of the plan. Use the consensus method for making changes, implementing strategies, or making decisions. Encourage and uphold one another in Christian love. Think of the other person more highly than yourself. Maintain the unity of the Spirit of God. Love should be the motivating factor for all that you say and do.

The first session is usually the most challenging. Be encouraged; things will undoubtedly get better as the group forms and respond to the material. Remember that you are not alone. Jesus Christ promised to be with each person in ministry. Remember also that God has gifted you with spiritual gifts and empowered you with the Holy Spirit to do the work God has called you to do. God has sent the Holy Spirit to lead and guide you into an effective ministry.

Encourage your group to read each of the sessions and complete the questions before each class. The better the group is prepared, the livelier and stimulating the study will be. Good preparation is the key to good participation. Do not be afraid to challenge your group to be well prepared. As leaders, you are to model this behavior.

Do not forget to emphasize the importance of the scripture references that have been included for each session. They provide a biblical foundation for each of the healing stories presented in this resource. They were included to strengthen and to support our understanding of the subject matter. They also emphasize the biblical accuracy of the content. Read aloud the current scripture passage for each of the sessions.

Begin and end each session with prayer. Leave time before the close of each session to pray for the individual needs of the participants. There should be an elevated level of expectation for healing. The Healing Moments content should create an atmosphere for healing to take place for yourselves and others. These sessions should serve as a learning laboratory for healing prayer. The Holy Spirit is present to lead and to guide you to be God's instruments of healing. Remember that

Jesus said that we would do the things that He did and more incredible things than these (John 14:12).

Everything that you do should be soaked in prayer. Also, encourage and communicate regularly with members of the group. Make sure to contact those who miss class. Emphasize their importance and let them know they were missed.

If your goal is to make healing an intricate part of your congregation, always mentor someone to be able to lead this study. Remember that healing was central to the ministries of both Jesus and the early church.

Leaders Should Keep the Following Suggestions in Mind:

1. Read the text and answer the question for each of the sixteen Healing Moments.
2. A vast amount of information and illustrations have been provided in each of these sections: Contemplation, Background, Encouragement, and Going Deeper. These sections are designed to enrich your talking points, provide essential information to support the subject matter, assuring that you make this learning experience the absolute best it can be.
3. Model openness, integrity, and warmth.
4. Keep all discussions open and lively. Remember to incorporate humor, especially when sessions seem to be too intense. Remind the group that God gives us the gift of joy and laughter.
5. Encourage reluctant participants to contribute to the discussions; seek ways to prevent an individual from dominating the conversation.
6. Keep the group focused on experiences rather than academic debates.
7. Exercise stewardship of time.
8. Set up the meeting room to be attractive and functional before people gather. Arrange the seating so that it will be comfortable. Include access to persons with handicapping conditions.
9. Make sure that the participants have a copy of the textbook at least a month before the first session, including a Bible.

10. Bring your unique style to the group and use your own words in the presentations. Use biblical and contemporary stories to keep the sessions fresh and exciting.1

11. If we are still living with a Covid-19 pandemic, consider holding a Zoom conference to conduct the study. Currently, we are using Zoom for all church activities. My wife, Gloria and I are currently teaching Miracles of Healing in the Gospel of Mark via Zoom. Virtual and digital apps are an excellent way to bring people together to teach a Bible study, conduct a workshop, or other gathering opportunities.

12. Feel free to adapt the suggestions to meet the needs of your group. Although one person can lead a group, having two leaders connect different ministry gifts for the good of all participants. Jesus used the team approach for leadership. You cannot go wrong following Jesus' example!

The answers that have been provided for the questions in each of the sixteen Healing Moments have been thoughtfully considered. They are not the only possible answers. You are to seek the wisdom and guidance of the Holy Spirit, and strive to come up with the best possible response to each of the questions, as I did. If my answers are helpful, then use them. But do not use them as a means for not doing your research and study to come up with the best possible answers. As author, I am a member of your team.

I hope that this leader's guide will be a blessing to you and your study group. My prayers will be with you all! Please send me your feedback and consider writing a review of the leader's guide.

The Healing Power of Jesus' Words

Key Concepts

Healing Moment One, "The Healing Power of Jesus' Words," demonstrates that his teaching and words carried the weight of God's power and authority. In casting out the uncleaned spirit (demon) shows that the kingdom of God has broken into human history. According to Jesus, healing is a sign that the kingdom of God has come near (Matt. 10:7-8).

Mark answered the question, "Why do bad things happen to good people." Jesus named Satan, as the veiled evil, behind the bad things. He did not debate the issue or ring his hands over it. Mark shows that Jesus' first public ministry action confronted Satan, exposing and overthrowing his evil work with the power of his words. Using the powerful words of Scripture, Jesus also demonstrated in the wilderness, his mastery over Satan's cunning lies and evil influence, in trying to prevent God's redemptive and kingdom work from being done (Luke 4:4-12 NIV).

As Jesus commands and drives the uncleaned spirit from the man, the people were amazed at Jesus' authority to command unclean spirits, and they obey him. Seeing and witnessing this phenomenon, they questioned who Jesus is, and where his authority had come from.1 Mark makes it clear that healing is a demonstration of God's kingdom work in the person of Jesus Christ. It was also evident of the dismantling of Satan's kingdom of darkness. The coming of the kingdom of God is a paradigm shift in human history.2

Let us be clear, Jesus' first public ministry act of confronting Satan and the demonic world was predicted long ago. This decision was made in the Garden of Eden when God executed the course of action to deal with the sin of Adam and Eve, which brought God's judgment against them, and the serpent (Gen. 3ff.NRSV). God decided the woman's seed would bruise the serpent's (Satan) head for deceiving Eve. The Scriptures point to Jesus as that Seed. Mark reports over and over that Jesus was chosen and anointed by God to resolve this conflict between God and Satan.3 God initiated the resolution of this conflict, putting it into motion, on God's terms, to be achieved in God's way, to satisfy God's righteous justice.

Mark's Gospel includes several exorcism incidents, emphasizing the continuous conflict between Satan's demonic evil work and Jesus Christ's redemptive mission. Mark also showed that Satan knows his kingdom is ending. As a created angel, he and his fallen angels are under God's power and control. They cannot do anything unless God allows it. As a fallen angel, Satan has chosen as his purpose on earth to prevent, distort, or destroy people's relationship with God.4

Although there is much evil influence in the world, we can rest assured that God is not sitting idly or silently by, while evil seems to prevail. God is in control and will bring an end to all manner of evil: sin, sickness, and death. Now, the Church, the body of Christ must continue the kingdom work of Jesus Christ in both the Church and world, until his return.

The Healing Power of Jesus' Words

Discovery

1. What about the healing of the man possessed by an unclean spirit is so significant as Jesus' first action to begin his public mission as the Messiah, the Son of God?

    A. It is noteworthy that the Gospel of Mark records a public exorcism of a man with an unclean spirit in a synagogue as Jesus' first ministry act. This was significant in several ways. First, God makes good on the promise that the seed of woman (Jesus, the Messiah of God) would bruise the head of the serpent (Satan) for his diabolical role in deceiving Eve to disobey God's warning not to eat the fruit from the tree of good and evil, which led to the Fall (Gen. 3 NIV). Second, the casting out of the demon demonstrated the power of Jesus' word over demons. Third, Mark showed that the demon recognized Jesus as the Holy One of God. Fourth, the demon knew Jesus had come to destroy the works of Satan, revealing that their malicious activities and influence in the world would come to a destructive end.

Fifth, this healing by exorcism looked back to the creation story of the Fall, but also looks toward the cross, witnessing to the coming of God's kingdom reign, and restoration of the Fall of humanity, including God's good creation.

2. When Jesus demonstrated his authority over demons, what did the people who witnessed it learn about him? How is this important for the church?

   A. The demonstration of Jesus' power and authority over demons shows that God's kingdom reign has broken into human history. God sent Jesus into the world to reveal God's reign and God's stance against Satan's evil works. Jesus has transferred God's power and authority to the church to continue Jesus' kingdom work in the world until his return.

3. What do demons know about Jesus that surprised you?

   A. It was surprising to learn how much knowledge demons had concerning the divine nature, character, power, and Jesus' relationship with God. It was also surprising to realize that everything demons knew about Jesus show us that they saw themselves as being inferior to Jesus and must obey his every word and action.

4. How is this healing miracle a significant change for the Kingdom of Satan and the Kingdom of God?

   A. Jesus' power over demons reveals that Satan's kingdom is ending, and that God's kingdom reign is being revealed.

5. What does this miracle tell us about God's attitude concerning sickness and human brokenness? (See Acts 10:38 NRSV.)

   A. It is essential to understand that sin, sickness, and spiritual death were not present in God's good creation. They were introduced into God's creation through the sin and disobedience of Adam and Eve in the Garden of Eden, including Satan's role in it all (Gen. 3ff).

6. Is God's authority over demons available to Christian believers today? (See Mark 3:13-19; Luke 9:1-2; 10:17-20; 1 Cor. 12:10 NRSV.)
   A. Yes! Each of the synoptic gospels tells us that Jesus has given the church God's power and authority to continue his kingdom work to heal the sick, cast out demons, cleanse lepers, and to raise the dead (Matthew 10; Mark 6; Luke 9-10 NRSV).

7. Who in your church do people turn to when they suspect demon activity in their own life or that of a loved one?
   A. Many of the mainline-denominational churches do not actively practice exorcism. Therefore, if people suspect demon activity, they might turn to the Roman Catholic church for help. Some charismatic and Pentecostal churches believe and practice healing by casting out of demons. Exorcism or casting out of demons is a vital, practical, and necessary ministry of healing in the Christian Church, which must not be denied or neglected.

8. What role should the church play in the practice of deliverance? (See Matt. 10:1-2, 8-10; Mark 3:14-15; Luke 9:1-2; 10:8-9, 17-20; Acts 10:38; 1 Cor. 12:9 NIV.) As disciples of Jesus Christ, what does it mean to have God's power and authority to be able to set people free from demonic activities?
   A. Exorcism or casting out of demons was a vital, practical, and necessary ministry of the kingdom work of Jesus Christ and the early church. God has not changed. This ministry of healing should be as significant in the modern Christian Church as it was during the early church era.

9. How has God gifted and equipped the church to continue Jesus' ministry of healing to those oppressed by the devil?
   A. The apostle Paul points out that God has gifted the church with spiritual healing gifts designed to bring healing and wholeness to broken humanity. God has given the church specific gifts to defeat demons, such as: discerning of spirits, wisdom, knowledge, faith, miracles, and gifts of healing.

10. Describe what you will take away from this healing moment that has given you hope and assurance that Jesus has defeated all our enemies, including demonic oppression.

   A. As the church takes seriously the spiritual power and authority God has given to the church, the body of Christ, believers are obligated to discover or rediscover how to use that power to liberate those oppressed by the devil (Matt. 10:1-2, 8-10; Mark 3:14-15; 6:12-13; Luke 9:1-2; 10:8-9, 17-20; Acts 10:38; 1 Cor. 12:9 NIV.)

HEALING MOMENT TWO

God's Amazing Healing Grace

Key Concepts

Healing Moment Two, "God's Amazing Healing Grace,' reveals that the exorcising of demons from people is a major theme of the synoptic gospels. Mark shows a continuous conflict between Jesus and Satan. He emphasizes that God has endowered Jesus with His power and authority over Satan and his demonic forces.

Mark also points out that demons knew more about Jesus than the people in the synagogue or the religious leaders. He identified Jesus Christ humanity, naming him as "Jesus of Nazareth.' The demon furthered recognized Jesus' deity, referring to him as "the "Holy One of God.' It is interesting that the demon revealed his fear of Jesus, knowing who he was, and that he had the power to both judge him, and to send him out of that area. Jesus quickly silenced the demon, from further revealing who he is.[1]

Mark shows that Jesus not only speaks for God, but also acts for God. Shortly after that confrontation with the unclean spirit, Jesus transferred God's power and authority to his disciples to heal the sick, cast out demons, cleanse the lepers, and even to raise the dead, as he had done.

The healing ministry of Jesus is about to shift into high gear. After leaving the synagogue, Jesus and his disciples accompanied Peter to his home. Arriving there, they learn that Peter's mother-in-law is in bed with a life-threatening fever (Luke 4:38-41NRSV). Telling Jesus of her dire condition, Jesus takes her by the hand and rebukes the fever. The fever immediately leaves her, and she gets out of bed and prepares a meal for Peter and his guests.

The healing of Peter's mother-in-law quickly spreads throughout the region. In the evening, when the sun had set, people from around the region come there to be healed by Jesus. Jesus heals many people and casts out many demons. The people experienced God's amazing healing grace. The news about Jesus' fame quickly spreads far and wide.

God's Amazing Healing Grace

Discovery

1. Read about this healing story in the gospels of Matthew (8:14-17) and Luke (4:38-41). Make notes of their differences and similarities.
    A. The healing of Peter's mother-in-law is reported in all the synoptic gospels. We need to hear what doctor Luke has to say about her condition. Doctor Luke describes the medical condition of Peter's mother-in-law as an extremely high fever. In other words, she had a life-threatening illness. A high fever tells us that her fever was 100 degrees or higher. Notice that she was in bed, which could mean that she was very weak, and suffering with a headache and pain. These are some of the signs or symptoms of a high fever: chills and shivering, severe headaches and muscle aches, a stiff neck, loss of appetite, irritability, dehydration, difficulty breathing or chest pain, mental confusion, or sweating.

2. Mark packed the healing of Peter's mother-in-law with much hidden and interesting information. Use your detective skills to see how much you can uncover.

    A. Mark made the healing of Peter's mother-in-law personal and quite captivating. The people in the house were very concerned for her health. They immediately told Jesus about her serious health condition. Jesus took her by the hand and rebuked the fever. The mother-in-law was instantly healed. She immediately got out of bed and prepared a meal for them to show her appreciation and gratitude. This healing spread quickly into the nearby towns; prompting others to bring the sick in their towns to Peter's house to be healed by Jesus. Jesus cured many who were sick with various diseases, and cast out many demons. Because the demons recognized who he was, Jesus prevented them to speak.

3. What did Peter's mother-in-law teach us about how to show our thanks and gratitude to God for the many blessings He bestows on us through Jesus Christ?

    A. The healing of Peter's mother-in-law teaches us that we are always to give thanks and praise to God for God's many blessings. Further, it teaches us that we have been blessed to be a blessing to others.

4. Even the demonic realm recognized who Jesus was, and where he had come from. What blinded the eyes and minds of the people Jesus came to redeem from recognizing him as their Messiah, even though they had witnessed the miracles he had performed?

    A. Demons recognized God's power and authority operating in and through Jesus of Nazareth. The people were blinded by their unbelief as to who Jesus was, even though they had witnessed God's power and authority demonstrated through Jesus' healing miracles.

5. What would our world look and feel like without God's healing presence and grace?

    A. Without God's healing power, presence, and grace, our world would feel cold and indifferent to human suffering and pain. We would be left on our own. We would feel unloved, and God would seem distant and uncaring.

6. Is there a difference between sickness and demonic possession?

    A. Jesus attributed sickness and demonic possession to Satan's evil influence. Both can be attributed to the results of sin in one sense. Satan's evil power is behind both. Let us not forget that the Fall of humanity, sin, sickness, and spiritual death were introduced into God's good creation.

7. Knowing that the sin problem has been atoned for through the cross, what sin in your life prevents you from experiencing God's healing grace?

    A. There are many obstacles to God's healing grace. In my booklet, *What Everyone Should Know About Healing*, I list seven obstacles that could prevent a person from experiencing God's healing grace. They are unbelief, fear, unworthiness, unforgiveness, ignorance, unresolved grief, and sin.

8. Jesus healed all the people who were brought to him with a word or touch. How has Jesus healed you?

    A. Through Jesus' atoning death on a cross, Jesus paid our sin debt; a debt we could never pay. Our salvation is the greatest healing anyone will ever experience. Through the cross, God has made forgiveness possible; and our broken relationship with God has been healed and restored. We are no longer God's enemies. Because of Jesus' redemptive work, we can become children of God, co-heir with Jesus Christ. Through the cross, God's image and likeness have been restored. We have passed from death to life. We have been delivered from darkness and translated into the marvelous light of Christ Jesus.

9. Why did the townspeople wait until the sun went down to bring the sick to be healed by Jesus?

    A. The Jewish Sabbath is from Friday evening to Saturday evening. They waited until the Sabbath was over. After the sun went down on Saturday, the crowds were free to bring their sick to be healed by Jesus.

10. What role does faith play in the healing process?

    A. Faith is essential in the healing process. If you do not believe a particular thing will happen it will not occur. You must have faith that Jesus can heal you. Your faith is placed in Jesus' ability to heal you. On numerous occasions, Jesus told several individuals. "Your faith has made you well" (Mk. 10:50NIV)." Or "Let it be done according to your faiths" (Matt. 9:29 NIV).

11. How are you caring for the physical and spiritual wellbeing of the elderly in your family, church, and the community?

    A. Both the Old and New Testaments instruct God's people to care for the elderly, widows, orphans, the sick, and the poor in our community. Serving those in need is the responsibility of all Christians (Zech. 7:10; Mal. 3:5; Matt. 25:31 to 46; James 1:27).

HEALING MOMENT THREE

Jesus Identifies with Human Brokenness

Key Concepts

Healing Moment Three, "Jesus Identifies with Human Brokenness," reminds us that healing is in the atonement. According to the prophet Isaiah, Jesus took our sins and sicknesses in his own body, as the eternal lamb of God, which were nailed to the cross. This healing story reminds us that by touching the leper, Jesus identified with the leper's humanity and brokenness. The healing miracles remind us of God's providential care toward humanity.

The healing of the leper tells us more about the compassion of Jesus than any other healing miracle found in the four gospels. For Jesus, touching the leper superseded the ceremonial rituals commanded by the law of Moses. In touching the leprous man, Mark allows us to see into the very heart and compassion of Jesus. His touch removed any doubts and fears the man may have had and reassured him of Jesus' willingness to heal him. Jesus' touch did not just heal the man physically, but healed him emotionally and spiritually at the very core of his being. (See Lev. 13:1-3 NIV.)

By touching the leper, Jesus risked becoming ceremonially unclean. Jesus' touch allowed the leper to experience the depth of God's love, mercy, and grace. His touch demonstrated that people are more important than man-made rules and laws.

Jesus Identifies with Human Brokenness

Discovery

1. What do the leper's words and gestures communicate to Jesus about his urgent desire to be healed?
   A. Leprosy was a very transmittable and infectious skin disease. The leper desperately wanted to be healed. He was willing to risk everything, even in making Jesus ceremonially unclean. Kneeling at Jesus' feet showed humility and reverence to Jesus. He believed that Jesus had the power to make him clean, but doubted in his heart if Jesus would heal him.

2. If leprosy makes a person ceremonially unclean, why do you think Jesus felt it was necessary to touch the leper before healing him?
   A. Jesus touched the leper to demonstrate that he was more important than men's laws and traditions. Second, Jesus' touch communicated both love and compassion to the leper. Third, by touching the leper, Jesus helped the leper feel human again. Finally, Jesus' touch removed all doubt of his intent to heal the leper.

3. From the leper's point of view, make a list of the significance of Jesus touching him.
   A. Jesus' touch demonstrated both love and compassion. It also showed the value and worth of the leper's personhood.

4. How was Jesus' method of healing the leper shocking to the leper, the disciples, and those who witnessed it?
   A. By touching the leper, Jesus risked becoming ceremonially unclean. As the Messiah of God, Jesus' mission was to set the captives free and bring healing, wholeness, and salvation.

5. The Prophet Isaiah tells us that a servant of the Lord *"has borne our infirmities and carried our diseases"* (Isaiah 53:4a NRSV). Do you think Jesus may have had this prophecy in the back of his mind when he touched the leper? Explain.
   A. Yes! For Jesus, healing and salvation are the two sides of the same coin. Jesus' death on the cross atoned for both human sins and their consequences.

6. Do your words and deeds conform to God's standard of loving your neighbor as you love yourself?
   A. Our words and deeds should mirror to others how God has treated us; by showing divine love, mercy, and compassion.

7. Under what circumstance have you humbled yourself before Jesus?
   A. As Christians, our aim is always to humble ourselves before God in every situation. The Bible reveals that in every generation, God has proven to be faithful and trustworthy, promising never to leave or to forsake us.

8. When Jesus looked at the leper and touched him, did he see his humanity before seeing his diseased conditioned?
   A. Yes! Jesus saw the leper's humanity before he saw his diseased conditioned. By touching the man, Jesus restored his humanity, and then he healed his disease. Jesus always intends to heal the whole person, spirit, body, mind, and soul.

9. When you ministered to others in Christ's name, how has Jesus' treatment of the leper informed you concerning how to pray for the sick and the oppressed?

    A. Jesus informs us to focus on the person and not on the disease. He also tells us that our presence is just as significant as our healing prayer. The aim of healing prayer is to create an atmosphere of healing grace. Christian healing prayer connects human need to God's healing power. Healing is a sign that God's kingdom has broken into human history!

10. In Jesus' day, society referred to lepers as unclean. What did Jesus convey to sociality and us by touching the leper?

    A. As mentioned above, Jesus was focused on the personhood of the leprous man. Jesus separated the person from his condition. Jesus' touch focused on the man's humanity and human dignity.

11. Describe what you will take away from this healing moment that has helped change your perspective about those marginalized today?

    A. In healing this man, Jesus not only restored his health but also restored him to his family, synagogue, and community. Healing is about restoration. Jesus demonstrated that healing touch is both therapeutic and transformative.

HEALING MOMENT FOUR

The Healing Power of Forgiveness

Key Concepts

Healing Moment Four, "The Healing Power of Forgiveness," empha sizes the importance of forgiveness. Jesus' healing of the paralytic man witnesses to the fact that God looks beyond our faults and sees our need for healing, wholeness, and salvation. Restoring our relationship with God and to each other is one of the ways people may experience healing, personally, and corporately.

Forgiveness is a powerful way to experience healing that may otherwise elude us. The healing of the paralytic gives us hope that forgiveness is possible. In forgiving the paralytic of his sins, Jesus opened the way for him to experience God's amazing healing grace. The Pharisees and scribes had a head knowledge of the Jewish sabbath law but knew nothing about grace. Understanding grace requires heart and spiritual knowledge. They did get one thing right—only God can forgive sins. However, they failed to see the incarnation of God manifested in the words and deeds of Jesus Christ. In the healing of the paralytic, they failed to see a demonstration of God's love, grace, and mercy that heals and liberates. Forgiveness is God's gracious gift to humanity that opens the way to healing, wholeness, and ultimately to salvation.

The Healing Power of Forgiveness

Discovery

1. What lesson do the four men teach us about faith and servant ministry?

    A. They teach us about the importance of loving our neighbor. They also teach us about faith, commitment, and perseverance. Further, they teach us that we should be an advocate for the sick and those in need. Furthermore, these men teach us that God wants people to be well and whole. Finally, they teach us that all things are possible with God.

2. Why didn't someone at the house where Jesus was teaching make room for the person with paralysis to be brought inside to be healed?

    A. Unfortunately, even today, many Christians tend to think only of their own needs. The people wanted to be near Jesus and did not want to lose their place near him. Mark points out that there was no room in the house because people were standing outside the home and peering through windows.

3. Why wasn't Jesus put off by the commotion created by the four men tearing through the roof and letting down the paralytic man in front of him?

   A. Jesus loved people as his heavenly Father did. He knew that God desired their highest good. Jesus always looked for ways to connect people's needs with God's power to make them whole. Jesus even marveled at the four men's faith and perseverance and rewarded their faith by healing the paralytic man.

4. Does the healing of the person with paralysis suggest that all sickness is the result of sin?

   A. By no means! Jesus dealt with this matter concerning the healing of the blind man found in each of the four Gospels (see Matt. 9:27-31; Mark 10:46-52; Luke 18:35-42; John 9:1-10:2 NIV). In John's Gospel, Jesus' disciples asked him why this man was born blind? "Was it because of his sin or the sins of his parents?" He rejected the connection with the disciples' erroneous theology between sinful actions and sickness. He taught them that not all illness was associated with sin. Jesus emphatically answers, *"Neither this man nor his parents sinned"* Jesus said, *but this happen so that the work of God's might be revealed in his life""* (John 9:1-3 NIV). Jesus tells his disciples that God healed the man because the need motivated the miracle and not the cause. We must remember that sin and illness were introduced into God's good creation (Gen. 1-3:24 NIV). According to God's word, Satan is the veiled evil behind most sickness, sin, and human brokenness in the world (Acts 10:38NIV).

5. Why is forgiveness essential to wholeness, freedom, and relationships?

   A. Forgiveness is an expression of God's unconditional love, a combination of divine mercy and grace. Jesus' redemptive death on the cross makes forgiveness possible. Forgiveness is at the heart of the gospel of salvation. In Psalm 103:1-3 NIV, the psalmist, King David, clarifies that God did not deal with him as his sins deserved. David reminds us that God deals with human beings out of the abundance of divine love and compassion. God not only forgives all our sins but also heals all our diseases. Because of this, we should always give thanks and praise for God's goodness, and mercy. It is essential to understand that healing and salvation are inseparable. Salvation is the ultimate healing. Finally, forgiveness reminds us that we must be a part of our healing process.

6. Put yourself in the place of the person with paralysis. What do you hear and feel when Jesus says to you: "*Son (daughter), your sins are forgiven* (Mark 2:4-5 NRSV)?

    A. When the paralytic heard Jesus say to him, "*Son, your sins are forgiven"* (Mark 2:5 NRSV) must have been both liberating and healing. As did the person with paralysis, I would immediately pick up my mat and walk, and give God praise and adoration for God's love shown to me through Jesus Christ!

7. What correlation does Jesus' forgiving the paralytic's sin have to do with the healing of his body?

    A. By forgiving the person with paralysis of his sins, Jesus healed him physically. The root cause of his condition was spiritual in nature. In this case, Jesus saw a correlation between his sin and his paralytic's physical condition. Forgiving the paralyzed man shows the spiritual nature of healing. It is important to understand that the healing of the paralyzed man also give evidence that sin is an obstacle to God's healing process.

8. Why do you think no one at the house offered to help the four friends get their paralyzed friend to Jesus to be healed?

    A. The house is overcrowded, where Jesus is teaching. The porch and the area around the house are also overflowing with by-standers.

    The people had gathered to hear Jesus teach and to witness Jesus performing miracles, which they did not want to miss.

The people inside the house were probably not aware of the four men carrying a man on a stretcher. If they had to move about, to make room for the person with paralysis, they may have thought that they would create a disturbance. There inactions showed the motives of their hearts and minds. They may have been thinking, "And the show must go on."

9. Is forgiveness something you struggle with, either to receive or to give? (See Matthew 6:9-15; 1 John 1:9-10; James 5:16 NIV.)

   A. Forgiveness is one of the most confusing and misunderstood spiritual principle to practice. Because of the destructive and spiritual nature of sin, and the complexity of the human personality and emotional makeup, many individuals struggle with forgiveness. Further, forgiving others is hard and complicated because of the emotional pain and hurt that are involved. Although, forgiveness is an act of the will, divine love, grace, and mercy are essential in the healing process.

10. Read the scripture passages: Psalm 103:12; Isaiah 38:17; 43:25; Jeremiah 31:34; Micah 7:9; Colossians 2:13-14. How completely does God forgive repentant sinners?

    A. Paul tells the Christians in Colossae, and us, that God has forgiven us of all our sins (Col. 2:13c NIV). The psalmist tells us that our heavenly Father does not deal with us according to our sins and that God has removed our sins as far as the east is to the west (Psalm 103:12- 13 NIV). That means God has eradicated human transgression from the universe; one commentator reminds us. Those who have put their trust in the atoning death of Jesus Christ will stand before God in the great judgment, free from sin, because of the redemptive power of the cross. The power of our sins was dealt with entirely through the cross.

11. Describe what you will take away from this healing moment that has helped change your perspective about your understanding of forgiveness and how you will use it to walk in freedom and peace?

   A. The Bible reminds us that terrible things happen to good people. Someone has said, "Two wrongs don't make a right, but they make a good excuse." When we practice forgiveness, we are living on the side of divine grace. Forgiveness is a means of grace, which is the way of the cross. Forgiveness brings both healing and peace to those involved in the conflict.

HEALING MOMENT FIVE

Healing is Always Lawful

Key Concepts

ealing Moment Five, "Healing Is Always Lawful," reveals that it is always right to do good. Jesus reminded the Pharisees that doing good should always supersede human traditions. He admonished the religious leaders for their strict interpretation of the sabbath law. He reminded them that the sabbath was made for man and not the other way around.

Mark tells us that on another sabbath, Jesus went into the synagogue as was his custom. His attention was drawn to a man with a withered hand. Some of the attendees watched him closely to see if he would heal the man on the sabbath. Jesus had the man stand up in front so everyone could see him. Having their attention, Jesus asked them a profound question, *"Which is lawful on the sabbath: to do good or to do evil, to save life or to kill"* (Mk. 3:4 NIV). Because the people remained silent, Jesus looked at them in anger and disgust.

Mark wanted his readers to see the healing miracles as living proof that good triumphs over evil. The miracles of Jesus clearly show that all manifestations of human suffering are evil and must always be confronted and eradicated. Mark further revealed that demonic activity was the primary source behind most human suffering and the evil in the world. Having made the connection between human suffering and evil, Jesus made the case that it is always justified and lawful to do good works, even on the sabbath. When Jesus confronted the people about working on the sabbath, their silence convinced him that the religious leaders were holding their tradition on a standard with God's Word.1

Healing is Always Lawful

Discovery

1. What made Jesus extremely upset with the people's response to his question concerning whether it was lawful to heal on the sabbath?

    A. It is clear, that many of the religious leaders had determined that Jesus was an enemy of their religious institution. They were jealous of his popularity. Jesus was a threat to their status in the synagogues, with the people and the community, diminishing their opportunity for personal gain. Further, Jesus humiliated them because he understood the Jewish Law and could teach it better than they could. Jesus could perform miracles to back up what he taught and spoke. Jesus could persuade the opinions of the people. Finally, Jesus rejected their interpretation of the law of Moses concerning the Sabbath.

2. How does the healing of the man with the withered hand differ from the previous four healings?

   A. The healing of the man with the deformed hand exposed the Pharisees' and other religious leaders of their religious hypocrisy and uncaring hearts. They had put their man-made traditions above the health and wellbeing of their fellow human beings.

3. Why do you think Jesus was more concerned with healing the man's withered hand than with being religiously correct?

   A. First, it is important to note that Jesus never broke one of the Jewish laws, for any reason. Jesus makes it clear that the needs and wellbeing of human beings is God's first, and ultimate priority. Jesus teaches that the traditions of man should never supersede the health and wellness of humanity. God sent the world a Messiah that both heals and saves.

4. How did Jesus challenge the paralyzed man's faith?

   A. All of the events leading up to the healing of the man with a deformed hand, were designed to build faith in him, and to challenge the religious leaders. Jesus challenged the man's faith by showing a personal interest in his physical condition. Jesus' expression of compassion toward the man was to give him hope of being healed.

5. In what way did the miracles done on the sabbath challenge the religious leader's literal interpretation of the sabbath and work done on the sabbath?

   A. I believe thar Jesus' double question was designed to achieve three things. First, Jesus challenged the motives of their hearts. Second, he challenged the biblical integrity of their interpretation of their Old Testament Scriptures, as they pertained to the love of neighbor and the sabbath law. Third, Jesus revealed that their keeping of the sabbath had not made them more spiritual or moved them any closer to God.

6. Read Mark 2:27-28. How does Jesus make his case that it is always lawful or right to do good works on the sabbath?

    A. These words of Jesus were an indictment to the Pharisees: *"The Sabbath was made to meet the needs of people, and not people to meet the requirements of the Sabbath. So, the son of man is Lord, even over the Sabbath"* (Mk. 2:27-28 NLT). God created the Sabbath for our benefit, restoring us both physically and spiritually. (See Samuel 21:1-6; Exodus 34:21; Leviticus 12:9-10; Deuteronomy 23:25.)

7. What religious tradition do you practice that puts you at odds with Jesus Christ and God's kingdom work?

    A. Unfortunately, I do not keep or practice God's Sabbath rest as I should or as God intended. However, in the future, I plan to start practicing the Sabbath rest. For most of my life, I have forfeited the benefits of God's blessing by not including the Sabbath as an intricate part of my spirituality. God also rested on the sabbath in order to bless and to restore God's people.

8. What was really behind the Pharisees attitude of wanting to kill Jesus for doing good on the Sabbath?

    A. The Pharisees believed that Jesus was a present threat to them keeping the status quo. Jesus was a threat to their financial, political, and social status in the community. They are like our corrupt religious and political leaders of today.

9. Why is healing always lawful on the Sabbath?

    A. God sees all forms of human brokenness as evil and destructive. God sent His Son, Jesus, to restore His good creation. In God's new creation there will be no sin, sickness, evil or death.

10. What do you think Jesus' motive was in reminding the Pharisees that the *"The son of man is the Lord of the Sabbath"* (Mark 2:27-28 NRSV)?

    A. Jesus was communicating to the Pharisees that the intent of God's law was to promote love for God and others. When those who claim to be God's servants and do not strive to fulfill the Great Commandment, they neither know nor love God. Those who love as God loves are born of water and the Spirit. Genuine born-again people not only love God but also love their neighbors. Listen to what John the Evangelist states, "*If someone says, I love God, but hates a Christian brother or sister, that person is a liar; For if we do not love people we can see, how can we love God whom we cannot see (1 John 4:20 NLT)?* Finally, Jesus wanted the Pharisees to understand that the real test of our love for God, is how we treat the people right in front of us— our family members and fellow believers. Life with God is a life of love and concern for those whom God loves.

11. Describe what you will take away from this healing moment that has helped to change your perspective about your view of the Sabbath law handed down by Moses?

   A. The life of the believer is a life of love and service. Living the Christian life is a life of love for God and others. This kind of life, "we cannot fake it until we make it." Jesus said that the world will know his disciples or followers by their love, period (John 13: 35)!

Jesus Empowers His Disciples to Heal

Key Concepts

Healing Moment Six, "Jesus Empowers His Disciples to Heal." Jesus invites his disciples to accompany him on a mountainside. There, he gives them an overview of the state of his ministry. To their surprise, and perhaps alarm, Jesus tells them that they are about to share in his ministry— the kingdom work of God. Jesus surprised them by appointing them as his apostles, symbolizing the twelve tribes of Israel. They would now participate up close and personal in the day-to-day operation of his ministry. By appointing them to engage in God's kingdom work, Jesus would receive the help that he desperately needed. Engaging them in his ministry would be a game changer.

Jesus trained, empowered, and used this ragtag group of men to continue his kingdom work after he had completed his earthly mission and returned to his heavenly Father. Before he sends them out, Jesus conferred his power and authority to them, which God had bestowed on him. The commissioning of this exclusive group of twelve apostles represented the creation of the infant church (Eph. 2:20 NIV).

Jesus Empowers His Disciples to Heal

Discovery

1. What were the apostles feeling and thinking when Jesus told them they would be sent out before him, to engage in his ministry of preaching and healing?

    A. Initially, the disciples felt a sense of pride, thinking that they were privileged to be called to be with Jesus and be considered members of his inner circle. However, having been with Jesus for only a brief time, they must have felt overwhelmed, unprepared, and perplexed to be commissioned to be his authorized representatives. Regardless of our maturity, gifts, and abilities, it is a daunting task to be mentally and emotionally prepared to be commissioned by Jesus to share in his day-to-day mission and ministry personally. Having served as an ordained minister in the ministry of the church for over thirty-five years, I still feel unprepared and overwhelmed.

2. If you were invited to spend the day with Jesus, what would you talk to him about?
   A. If we think about it, as followers of Jesus Christ, it will depend on the kind of personal relationship we have with Jesus to define what we would talk to him about.

3. How much time do you spend with God, talking about the things that matter to God's kingdom work?
   A. Again, how much time we spend with God and talk about the things that matter to God may seem absurd to some people. Yet, serious-minded believers who have a deep personal relationship with God speak to God about many things. Spending time with and communicating with God should be an intricate part of every believer's personal life and spirituality.

4. How have you responded to God's call to Christian discipleship—servant ministry?
   A. As a Christian disciple of Jesus Christ, I consider it a privilege to be called into servant ministry; to serve and tell others about God's goodness, love, grace, and salvation.

5. What or who has helped prepare you to respond to God's call to servant ministry?
   A. Most of us, as I have, had a family member, friend, or pastor lead us to know God through Jesus Christ. And those relationships helped to ground and motivate us to trust God enough, to say yes to God's call to servant ministry.

6. Is there a correlation between faith and obedience concerning your response to the call of Christian discipleship?
   A. Faith and obedience are essential components concerning how each of us responds to the call to Christian discipleship. We live out our discipleship through our service to God and others.

7. Do you accept the premise that you can make a difference in the kingdom work of God? Why? Why not?

    A. Unless we believe that we can make a difference in God's Kingdom work, we will forever sit on the sideline of life, with many regrets and sorrows. By discovering our place in God's kingdom, we will embrace our humanity and purpose, making this world a little better.

8. Have you responded to God's call to follow Christ in advancing the work of the kingdom?

    A. Every person must discover why he or she exists. No human being was created without a purpose. God created each of us to advance God's Kingdom work. Our mission is to make the beloved community big enough to embrace all humanity.

9. Take a moment and think about your call to servant ministry. Using a scale from 1 to 5, with 5 being the practical side of ministry, how would you grade your servant ministry's effectiveness?

    A. This question requires both honesty and integrity. To make an honest assessment of your service to God, you will need the Holy Spirit's guidance and help. Whatever the outcome, use this as an opportunity to rededicate yourself to the Lord's service.

10. Read John 14:12. In what way does this statement of Jesus informs your Christian service?

    A. When Jesus said that his disciples would do the works of the kingdom as he had done, he fully anticipated that God would work in them, as he had worked in him, spreading the good news of the kingdom— the gospel of salvation.

11. Do you believe that one person can make a difference in the kingdom work of God?

    A. Yes! We only need to look at the life of Jesus Christ to know that one person can make a difference in God's kingdom work. When a person is dedicated to accepting the call to servant ministry, one person can make a difference, that has eternal consequences.

HEALING MOMENT SEVEN

Jesus' Power Knows No Bounds

Key Concepts

Healing Moment Seven "Jesus' Power Knows No Bounds," reveals that Jesus' ministry moved beyond the territory of the Jews to a place called Gerasene, a Gentile region. There, a small group of Jews lived. In Gerasene, Jesus encountered another situation involving an exorcism of a man with an unclean spirit. The demons restrained the man in a cemetery among the tombs; he was at their mercy. The presence of a legion of demons in the man gave him super-human strength. No humans could restrain the man, not even with iron shackles and chains. This shows that even the community was also under the control of the demons.

As we observe Jesus' kingdom work, it becomes increasingly clear that he is passionate about liberating all people from their suffering and bondage. Jesus gives this kingdom work to the church to continue after he returns to his Father. His last instruction to his followers was to proclaim the good news of the gospel of salvation— first, in our homes, then to our friends and acquaintances, next to our community, and finally to the world. (See Matt. 8:18-20; Acts 1:5-8 NIV.)

Jesus' Power Knows No Bounds

Discovery

1. Demons recognized Jesus as the Son of the Most High God. What prevented the leaders and the people from recognizing who Jesus was, even after observing his miracle-working power and authority over demons?

   A. No one had ever seen anyone like Jesus that freely demonstrated the power of God's authority over demons, sickness, and even death.

2. Why did the demons beg Jesus not to send them out of the area?

   A. The demons begged Jesus not to send them out of the region because they are territorial. This was their home. Some 3,000 to 6,000 demons (Legion) ruled over both their victims and that region of Gerasene.

3. In what ways were the demons in control of the community, and what was the significance?

   A. There are several tell-tell signs that the community was under the control of the Legion of demons. First, the people were powerless to cast out the evil spirit from the man. Second, the people's only response was to bind the man with chains and shackles as a means of keeping him from possibly hurting himself and from coming around people to make them ceremonial uncleaned, living among the tombs of dead people. Third, the people did not turn to Jesus to ask him to heal the man. Fourth, the region's believers did not seem to relate to the possessed man in any humane way.

4. What does the farming of pigs tell you about this region and the Jews living there?

    A. The farming of pigs tells us that this region is a Gentile and pagan area.

5. Jesus had now moved his mission to a Gentile territory outside of Galilee. Why is this significant?

    A. Jesus' mission was first to present the gospel of the kingdom to the Jews. However, his ultimate mission was to bring salvation to the entire world. The fact that Jesus was moving his mission to a Gentile region suggests that his earthly mission of spreading the good news of the kingdom was drawing near. His mission would not be over until the gospel of the kingdom had been planted among the Gentiles.

6. When the demon saw Jesus and bowed down before him, was this an act of worship?

    A. Although the demons recognized Jesus' divinity, power, and authority, they bowed down to him out of reverence and submission, not worship. Demons, in general, hated both God and Jesus and anyone who would accept and followed Jesus Christ as their Savior and Lord. They approached Jesus, hoping to persuade him not to send them away from the area where they had established control over their victims and the region.

7. What did the demon-possessed man learn about the severity of his condition after Jesus permitted the demons to enter the pigs?

   A. Jesus had the power and authority to send the demons out of the area or to hell. Rather than sending the demons out of the area, he granted their request to send them into the pigs. In doing so, Jesus demonstrated to the people of that region that he had absolute power over demons. He also showed the demon-possessed man and the people that God is no respecter of persons. Healing this Gentile man proved to them that God also loved them. They could turn from the kingdom of darkness to the kingdom of God. Finally, Jesus revealed to the man the severity of his condition by allowing the Legion of demons to enter the pigs.

8. How did Mark describe the mental condition of the man before and after Jesus healed him?

   A. Mark wanted his readers to know that Jesus heals the whole person. Not only was the man healed spiritually, but also mentally (emotionally) and relationally. Jesus sent the man back to his family and community, instructing the man to tell the people how much God had done for him.

9. Read Luke 9:1-2; 10:9; 10:17-20. Describe what Jesus wanted the disciples to understand about the authority they had over demons.

   A. In these passages of Scripture, Luke points out that God has given the followers of Jesus Christ the same power and authority over demons as God had given to Jesus Christ.

10. Is there a connection between the healing of the man and the drowning of the pigs?

    A. The connection between the healing of the possessed man and the drowning of the pigs shows that the kingdom of Satan is no match against God's kingdom. Further, no matter how big our problem, God's power is more significant.

11. By allowing the demons to enter the pigs, Jesus was illustrating something significant he wanted all the spectators to comprehend. What was displayed in the people's eyes that told the whole story of the coming kingdom of God?

     A. It seems reasonable that by allowing the demons to enter the pigs illustrated the supreme power of God's kingdom over demons. Second, God's presence and power are always available to people oppressed by Satan. Third, God's anointed Messiah has come to proclaim the good news of the kingdom to the oppressed, *"to bind up the brokenhearted, to proclaim liberty to the captive, and release to the prisoners; to proclaim the year of the Lord's favor, and the day of vengeance of our God, and to comfort those who mourn"* (Isaiah 61:1-4 NRSV).

HEALING MOMENT EIGHT

A Faith That Would Not Be Denied

Key Concept

Healing Moment Eight, "A Faith That Would Not Be Denied," points out that God rewards expectant and persistent faith. It also reminds us that God is not indifferent to the needs of humanity, no matter who you are. There is nothing too small or too hard for God to achieve. We can bring our insufficiencies to the all-sufficient Christ.

Mark reports on a woman who had suffered for twelve years with a life-threating bleeding or menstrual problem and Jairus's daughter who was near death. Mark reports that the woman had spent all the money she had on many doctors, but her condition got worse. Fortunately, for this woman, she alone with many of the people, had come to the beach that day and heard secondhand stories about Jesus' power to heal. Those stories became messages of hope and good news, strengthening and emboldening a faith within her that would not be denied. Jairus, a caretaker of a synagogue, probably had witnessed first-hand many healings that Jesus had performed.

Jesus had just arrived by boat back in a predominantly Jewish territory.

As soon as Jesus and his disciples had stepped out of the boat onto the beach, they were surrounded by a large crowd. Some of the people had come to hear Jesus teach. Several people in the crowd had come in hope to be healed by Jesus. Many of their circumstances were desperate because they were facing a life and death situation. Time was not on their side. They needed a blessing and breakthrough from heaven! They needed a miracle! They needed to be healed by Jesus Christ, and time was running out.

A Faith That Would Not Be Denied

Discovery

1. Who or what do you turn to when you are faced with a health crisis requiring immediate action?

    A. When faced with a health crisis requiring immediate action, most people often turn to the health care community if they have medical insurance. Otherwise, they deal with the problem on their own. Sadly, God is usually the last resource people turn to for help. The woman with the menstrual condition is the typical response of most people. If people only knew how much God and Jesus loved them, they would be one of the first to turn to Jesus in a crisis (See John 15; James 5:13-16).

2. Think of a situation when your faith seems smaller than the problem you face. To whom did you turn?

    A. People's answers will vary greatly. When our youngest daughter, Christina, was a baby, her pediatrician told us that she had an inguinal hernia. The hernia was very painful and caused her to cry often. At the time, our faith seemed small and insignificant. My wife and I cried out to God continually, but nothing happened. One night, Christina woke us up in the middle of the night, crying in pain. I felt compassion for her and lifted her to God and prayed this prayer of desperation: "Lord, if I could heal Christina, I would, but I cannot; but you can." Immediately, Christina stopped crying, and we all went back to sleep. From that night, Christina never cried again. However, several days later, we took Christina to the doctor to be checked for the hernia. To our surprise and amazement, the doctor could not find a hernia. That night, God heard our many prayers and healed our daughter. Forty some years later, Christina is still healed.

3. Where did the woman's first glimmer of hope come from, turning her sorrows and disappointments into hope and a joyful expectation?

   A. Hearing the many healings' stories Jesus had performed in various places, the woman's faith was greatly strengthened. She believed that if those people could be healed, she believed that she, too, would be healed. Acting on her faith in Jesus' power to heal her, she forced her way through the crowd and touched Jesus' clothes. Jesus rewarded her expectant and bold confidence. He said to her, *"Daughter, your faith has made you well. Go in peace, and be healed of your affliction"* (Mark 5:34 NKJV).

4. Why would Jesus spend so much time with this woman when Jairus's daughter faced a life and death crisis?

   A. Jesus always gave his presence and full attention to the person who needed God's help, as if their concerns were God's top priority. All our needs and concerns are personal to God. Further, Jesus makes it clear that God is in control and can meet every need of His humanity. The healing miracles of Jesus Christ demonstrated that God is a present help in a time of need. We can bring our insufficiencies to the all-sufficient God.

5. Which scripture comes to mind that gives you assurance God cares about the situations you face in your daily life?

    A. Psalms 103 gives me the assurance that God cares about the situations that I face in my daily life. The Bible has thousands of promises of God, which assures me of God's love and providential care that are always available to those who put their trust in the Living and gracious God. Through the cross, Psalm 103 reminds us that God has made provisions for all our physical and spiritual needs.

6. What other challenges did the woman face that threatened the quality of her life?

    A. Because of the length of this woman's illness, she had spent all her money on doctors, trying to find a cure for her illness. Also because of her prolonged physical condition, she had to live in isolation. The bleeding condition made her religiously unclean. She could not attend the synagogue or other opportunities to be in fellowship with the religious community. Having no money to take care of herself, this could have caused her to become homeless as well. Her only redeeming quality would be that she had other family members that could provide for her. The list goes on.

7. How have the healing miracles helped to strengthen your faith to be healed?

    A. All the healing miracles remind us that we are not alone, and that God is only a prayer away.

8. What compelled the woman to confess to Jesus that she was the person who touched his clothes?

    A. Jesus' response to the fact that healing power flowed out of him, and he was questioning who touched him, convinced her that Jesus knew that someone had been healed. Although she was amazed and shocked at the same time, she was under conviction to reveal to Jesus that she was the one who touched his clothes, releasing God's healing power and grace.

9. What did Jesus communicate to the woman by referring to her as "daughter"?

    A. When Jesus referred to the woman as "daughter," Jesus communicated that her personhood as well as her condition were important to his heavenly Father. By referring to her as daughter, Jesus revealed to her, and to us, that neither our diseases nor condition in life, define our humanity, but God does.

10. Recount a situation or circumstance in your life when you felt that if God had not responded quickly to your need, you would not have made it.

    A. Had God not intervened in my life and others, none of us would have made it.

11. Describe what you will take away from this Healing Moment that has helped you to face an uncertain future or a life-threatening situation?

    A. What I will take away from this Healing Moment is that God is on the side of all humanity, no matter what we might face on this side of the vail. We can always turn to God in times of trouble. Therefore, we should love and serve God with our whole being.

HEALING MOMENT NINE

Jesus' Supreme Power Over Death

Key Concepts

Healing Moment Nine, "Jesus' Supreme Power over Death," highlights Jairus's daughter being raised from the dead. If you have ever experienced a life-threatening illness of one of your children, you know the agony Jairus was going through. As a parent, you will do whatever it takes to get the best possible help to make your child well again. Jairus falls at the feet of Jesus and pleads fervently with him to come to his house and lay his hands on his young child, who was dying. Jairus seemed confident in Jesus' ability to save his daughter from her life-and-death struggle. Jairus puts his daughter's life into the Great Physician's hands— the Healing Messiah of God (Isa. 42:61).

This healing story assures us that not even death is beyond God's power to heal. When the leaders of Jairus' home synagogue came, bearing the shocking news that his daughter had died, Jesus said to them: *"Do not fear, only believe" (Mark 5:35 NRSV).* Jesus reminds Jairus and us that nothing, absolutely nothing, is impossible to God. As the Creator of the universe and all living things, God has the power and authority to raise the dead.

You may have heard this saying in the Christian community: "*God may not be there when you want him, but He's always on time.*" Jairus discovered that God is an on-time God. Jesus has said many things that has helped us get through challenging times, encouraging us not to lose hope, but to believe. I do not know of any situation or circumstance where Jesus did not offer people hope. The keyword he used to build faith and to give hope was *to believe*. To believe is to accept by faith the promises of God. We are not to waver in our faith concerning the promises of God. Healing is one of those promises.

Jesus challenged Jairus to believe and have faith in his ability to raise his daughter from the dead. Jesus offered Jairus hope and a promise. No matter what you are going through, God in Christ has the perfect solution.

Jesus' Supreme Power Over Death

Discovery

1. How would you describe Jairus's faith in Jesus' ability to heal his daughter, even in the face of death?
    A. Even after Jairus's daughter had died, Jesus encouraged Jairus to believe and not to doubt God's power to raise his daughter from the dead. It seems obvious that he had taken Jesus at His word, remaining confident and hopeful that the mere touch of Jesus' hand possessed God's power to heal his daughter. God rewards Jairus's expectant faith.

2. How would you describe expectant faith?
    A. Expectant faith does not waver even in the face of death. It believes that all things are possible with God.

3. Describe a time when Jesus came through for you.
    A. Early in my walk with God, God was directing our family to move from Delaware to Tulsa, Oklahoma, for me to attend graduate school at O.R.U. As we prepared to make this trip, we only had $117.00. Lacking the money necessary to take such

a long journey, we had significant concerns because we would have to make this trip with our six young children. Doing the math, we knew that we would need at least $300.00 to take this trip. Failing to acquire more funds to take the journey, we decided to trust God's providential care to meet our every need for this trip. We also agreed only to talk about our needs with our heavenly Father. We only stayed in a hotel one night. The rest of the time, God opened doors for our lodging in the homes of strangers and our parents. Without knowing our financial needs, God put it on strangers' hearts to bless us with gifts of money. While we were in Tulsa, we decided to visit Gloria's parents' in Lorman, Mississippi. They had not seen three of their grandchildren. After we arrived back in Delaware, having been on this trip for nine days, we brought groceries. Arriving home and emptying my pockets, we were amazed and profound, to discover that we had exactly $117.00, the amount of money that we had when we began that amazing trip.

4. How did Jesus respond to the news this Jairus's daughter had died?
   A. Jesus' response to the information that Jairus's daughter had died was for him to believe in his ability and power to heal his child. Jesus treated the death of the child as merely being asleep. Jesus let Jairus know that with God's power raising his daughter from death was like awakening her from sleep with God's power.

5. As Christians, how should we respond when we receive bad news?
   A. As Christians, our response is always to put our faith and trust in God's many promises. We should also keep in mind that God in Jesus Christ, promised never to leave or forsake us, regardless of the situation or circumstance.

6. Is there any biblical support in the Bible that informs believers in their expectation of the resurrection?

   A. Both the Old and New Testaments teach us that the resurrection is central to God's redemptive kingdom work. Jesus' own words and actions give us the most definitive proof that God has the power to raise the dead. Jesus made it clear to Jairus, the mother, and his three companions that for God, raising a person from the dead is as simple as awakening a person from sleeping. He simply takes the girls' hands and commands her to get up (Mark 5:41). In response to Jesus' touch and words, the girl gets up and walks about the room. When Jesus arrives at the tomb of his friend, Lazarus, his sister tells Jesus that if he had been there, he could have prevented his death. What happened at the tomb of Lazarus is profound. Jesus tells Martha what he had told Jairus to believe in God's power to raise the dead. But he goes further, revealing for the first time that he is Israel's Messiah, with these profound words: "*I am the resurrection and the life. Anyone who believes in me will live, even after dying. Everyone who lives in me and believes will never die. Do you believe this, Martha?*" (John 11:25 NLT) Then, Jesus commands Lazarus to come out of the tomb. Lazarus comes out of the tomb wearing grave clothes. The resurrection of the girl and Lazarus is the universal reality for those who believe in God's redemptive work in the cross.

7. What did Jairus's daughter and the woman with the issue of blood have in common?

   A. Jairus's daughter and the woman with hemorrhaging were both facing a life and death situation. Expectant faith in God's healing grace and power were the appropriate and necessary components that gave each of them a new lease on life. Each of them was dependent on divine grace. Each of them needed a miracle that only Jesus could provide. Both discovered that death is no harder for God to heal than any other illness or disease. Jairus and the woman found that with God, believers should never give in to despair or hopelessness because that which is impossible with human beings is possible with God. Finally, their healing displays the love and compassion of God, demonstrated powerfully in Jesus Christ, over illness, diseases, evil spirits, and now, death.

8. How are you to understand Jesus' use of the term sleeping when it refers to the dead?

   A. In this case, Jesus used sleep as an image or a metaphor for death. He used the word sleep to suggest that the dead girl's condition was temporary, and that she would be restored to life, as if, to be awakened from sleeping.

9. Why did Jesus not allow the people of Jairus home to accompany him in the room where he prayed for the dead girl? Explain.

   A. Jesus did not allow the mourners to accompany him into the room to raise the girl from death because their understanding and motives were focused on death, hopelessness, sorrow, and weeping. On the other hand, Jesus was motivated and focused on God's love, compassion, healing power, and life. The mourners would have conflicted with Jesus seeing that same situation of the girl's death from God's perspective of healing and restoration to life.

10. Describe what you will take from this Healing Moment that has helped change your perspective about death or dying.

    A. The thing I will take from this Healing Moment is the significance and power of faith. As I say in the book, we should never waver in our faith concerning the promises of God. God has never made a promise that He does not keep. Finally, bold, and expectant faith reminds us that nothing is impossible with God. When we do not have the answers to our problems, we should put our faith in God's wisdom, amazing love and healing grace.

HEALING MOMENT TEN

Jesus' Disciples As God's Healers

Key Concepts

Healing Moment Ten, "Jesus' Disciples as God's Healers," affirms that the Christian life is a shared life in Jesus Christ. Jesus hand-picked his twelve disciples and taught them how to serve as he served. He commissioned them and gave them the authority to preach repentance, heal the sick, and cast out demons as God had commissioned him to do. Jesus' twelve disciples modeled for us how to respond to God's call to servant ministry. They were Jesus' closest companions. They learned to serve as Jesus served. They learned to love the people that God loved. They developed a heart of love and compassion for people that mirrored the character and heart of Jesus.

Although the disciples were sold out for Jesus, the ministry revealed their human faults and failures. Despite the human failures and unbelief of his disciples, Jesus stuck with them through thick and thin. From time to time, they frustrated, disappointed, and angered Jesus, but he never gave up on them or stopped believing in them. Jesus chose ordinary people just like you and me. All the original twelve disciples, except the one destined to betray him, completed their mission in obedience and faithfulness.

Jesus fully anticipated that the church would continue his kingdom work, both in the church and the world (John 14:12). He gave the church two mandates to fulfill before his return, The Great Commandment, and the Great Commission. He sent the gift of the Holy Spirit for that very purpose. The church still has the mandate to go into the world and make disciples of all nations, baptizing them in the name of the Father, Son, and the Holy Spirit. Jesus Christ has given every disciple of every generation this promise, "...I am with you always, even to the end of the age" (Matt. 28:20 NRSV).

All baptized believers have been called and equipped to servant ministry as disciples of Jesus Christ. Our servant ministry is not to be neglected or to be taken for granted. No one else can do what God has called each of us to do. Our response to the call to servant ministry will have an eternal consequence in this world and the eternal kingdom of God.

First, and foremost, the servants of God should be spiritual persons. Servant ministry should be Spirit-empowered, Spirit-led, Spirit-gifted, and dedicated to continuing Christ's mission and ministry until his return.

Jesus' Disciples As God's Healers

Discovery

1. If God's power is unlimited, why wasn't Jesus able to heal but a few sick persons?

   A. God's power is not only unlimited, but there is also no power on earth, or in the heavens above, that can match God's power. God's power is supreme and is without limitations. Although Mark recorded that Jesus could heal only a few sick persons, this was not the central point of this incident. Mark's point was to emphasize the importance of faith in the healing process. Faith is the catalyst of all healing miracles. It is essential to understand that the unbelief of the people in that region, hindered them from being healed, but not Jesus' ability or power to heal them. By choosing to limit who he would heal, he confirmed Jesus' true motive for healing those few persons that had the faith to be healed. There is a difference between choosing not to heal and not having the power to heal. Remember, there were many people in the crowd, pushing against or touching Jesus. Just touching Jesus will not release his power to heal. However, when the woman touched Jesus, her touch was a sign of intentionality and purpose. Her faith caused the healing power to flow out of Jesus to be healed. She touched Jesus with her faith, as well as her hand.

2. There is no evidence that Jesus anointed the people he healed. Why did his disciples anoint with oil in their practice of healing?
   A. Mark, Luke, and the apostle James teach us that it was a customary practice of healing in the early church to incorporate the laying on of hands and the anointing the sick with oil (Mark 6:13; Luke 10:34; James 5:13-16 NIV). Anointing with olive oil was commonly used for medical purposes, as part of regular spiritual practices, and for acts of worship. Olive oil was the best medicine for that period. It was used as a medicine for both the physical and spiritual dimensions of human life. Jesus instructed the Pharisees not to fast simply to look spiritual or to get the approval of others. He encouraged those genuinely fasting to anoint their head with oil and wash their face (Matt. 6:17 NIV). Jesus' use of the oil was to remind the Pharisees of the spiritual nature of fasting as one of the spiritual disciplines, which he named as prayer, fasting, and the giving of alms. You may recall the parable that Jesus told his disciples about the parable of the Good Samaritan in Luke 10:30-37. In the parable, a gentile passerby came to the rescue of the man attacked and beaten by robbers. The Good Samaritan poured oil and wine on the man's wounds to express compassion and healing. King David speaks of God as his Shepherd, who protects and cares for him as one of his sheep. God anointed David's head with oil, when faced with his enemies and death (Psalm 23:1-6NIV). Oil is also a symbol of the Spirit of God, which was used to anoint kings (1 Sam.16:1-13 NIV). Before that, oil was used to anoint the Priests of Israel (Exodus 30:30 NIV).

3. If the people in his hometown did not take Jesus' ministry seriously, why would they take his disciples seriously?
   A. The disciples were Jesus' representatives. The people rejected Jesus' ministry because they were spiritually blind and could

not fully discern his messianic mission's nature and scope. They also rejected his ministry because they wanted to maintain their status, popularity, and power in the community. They considered Jesus as a threat to them, so they dismissed both his mission and message. Over time, the apostles gained the respect and support of most people and many of the religious leaders. God uses people to do His kingdom work, whether or not people accept the ministry or message of His servants.

4. What two things amazed the people about Jesus?
   A. The people were amazed at Jesus' teaching because he interpreted the Scriptures so that it made sense to them. The way Jesus taught them, the people could relate to his teachings, and they could apply them to their everyday lives. Second, the miracles that Jesus performed also amazed them. Jesus demonstrated power over sickness and disease. He exercised power over demons, nature, and death.

5. Why did Jesus send out the disciples in pairs of two?
   A. Jesus sent the disciples to do ministry in teams of two for practical reasons. First, two heads are better than one. Second, by nature, the ministry is a lonely task. Third, two persons would be a source of support and encouragement. Fourth, a two-person team brings together many gifts, skills, abilities, wisdom, and discernment to significantly impact the ministry's task. Fifth, we forget that the Christian life is a shared life in Jesus Christ. Sixth, a team approach to ministry is more effective.

6. Jesus sent out the disciples to preach and to heal from village to village. Why do you think he told them not to take any money, bread, or other personal items they might need while on the mission field?
   A. The primary reason Jesus instructed the disciples not to take money, bread, or other personal items, was because he wanted to teach them that they were to put their total trust in God's

protection and providential care. Whatever material goods we possess, God is the source of them all. On several occasions, Jesus told them that he could do nothing on his own. He did only what he saw the Father doing (John 15:19). The parable of the vine and the branches was told to reinforce this very point. Jesus taught a branch can only live and bear fruit if it abides in the vine. Jesus is that vine, and the disciples are the branches that must abide in the vine, to bear fruit that lasts (John 15:4-5 NIV). Finally, this parable teaches the importance of love and obedience.

7. Although the disciples were sent out to heal the sick, what was their mission's primary purpose?

    A. The primary purpose of the mission of Jesus' disciples was to proclaim the gospel of the kingdom of God, calling their Jewish people to repentance, and to accept the salvation of God.

8. What is the likelihood that you would have agreed to go out on an evangelistic mission as the disciples of Jesus without money, food, extra clothing, or prospects of a place to lodge at night?

    A. Most believers would question the wisdom of Jesus' instruction, thinking that this was not a wise decision. Having said this, Jesus' disciples faithfully and obediently fulfilled their mission, preaching a message of repentance, healing the sick, and casting out many demons. They trusted Jesus' wisdom, and because of their obedience, God worked through them with great power, giving them success, on their first mission.

9. Was there a specific lesson Jesus wanted his disciples to learn by sending them out on an evangelistic mission without any resources?

    A. Jesus used this first missionary opportunity of his disciples, to fortify their faith at the very beginning of their ministry. He used this mission trip as a life-lesson and as a powerful teaching moment. As his followers, Jesus wanted his disciples to discover for themselves that they could trust in God's providential care to meet their every need. Both Jesus and Paul taught the Christian community the importance of caring for and supporting those who lead and teach the body of Christ. (See Matt. 10:10; Luke 10:7; Gal. 6:6; 1 Tim. 5:18; Lev. 19:13.) In Luke 22:35, after the disciples had returned from their mission, Jesus asked them this poignant question: "*When I sent you out that time without purse, bag, or shoes, did you lack anything?" "Not a thing," they answered Lk. 22:35 NIV)?*. Bishop T. D. Jakes preached a message that crystalizes Jesus' lesson to his disciples and to us; "If God has called us to it, God will see us through it."

10. Describe what you will take away from this healing moment that has helped change your perspective about servant ministry.
   A. Servant ministry is a noble and high calling. It is a privilege to share in the mission and ministry of Jesus Christ, which we should never take for granted. As members of the body of Christ, we are God's agents of change. What we do for God has eternal consequences!

HEALING MOMENT ELEVEN

Healing Faith, Not Magic

Key Concepts

Healing Moment Eleven, "Healing Faith, Not Magic," makes the case that an unspiritual person cannot comprehend or accept spiritual matters. Even believers need the help or aid of the Holy Spirit to receive the things of God. Mark makes it clear that God responds to faith and not magic. Magic is manipulation that may give the appearance of faith and leads to all kinds of confusion and dependence on self, and not on God. God's love cannot be manipulated or earned. Healing is a means of grace. God heals because He loves humanity unconditionally. God desires and seeks our highest good.

Mark places several miracle incidents side-by-side in this healing moment, contrasting faith and unbelief as he had recorded elsewhere. God rejects unbelief but rewards faith. This is a lesson we should all learn from. God's rewards are often surprising. Mark points out that the disciples did not connect the dots of Jesus's miracles concerning his identity. The disciples did not understand the loaves and two fish miracles, Jesus' power to heal all manner of illnesses, his authority to cast out demons, and his power over nature, the wind, and the sea. In all these miracles, the disciples did not recognize Jesus as their anointed messiah. Their fears would lead to their failures to comprehend the things of God's kingdom work, until after the resurrection and the pouring out of the Spirit of God.

The news about the woman who touched the hem of Jesus' cloak and was miraculously healed had circulated near and far. This news had reached the shores of Lake Gennesaret, the north-western shore of the Sea of Galilee. The people in this region believed if this woman, who had been sick for twelve years, could be healed by touching Jesus' clothes, why would that not also work for them. We know that God rewards faith, even the faith as small as a mustard seed. The people decided to put their faith in Jesus' ability to heal them.

They put their faith into action by gathering all their sick, carrying them on mats, and laid them in the marketplaces. Wherever Jesus and the disciples went into the villages or countryside, the sick begged that they might touch his cloak. Those who touched his clothes were healed. God rewarded their expectant faith!

Healing Faith, Not Magic

Discovery

1. How would you describe the faith of those who were healed by touching Jesus' clothes?

    A. The people of this region had no personal experience of Jesus' healing ministry. However, they had heard stories of Jesus' power to heal. They had also heard of the healing of the woman that had been miraculously healed after touching the edge of Jesus' cloak. They put their faith into action by gathering all the sick and laying them in the town, villages, and farming communities so that they might touch the clothes of Jesus as he passed by.

2. Is this story of healing miracles more about magic than it is about faith? Explain.

    A. This is a story of faith and not magic. The people believed that just as the woman with the menstrual bleeding problem was healed by touching the hem of Jesus' cloak, they could apply their faith in the same way. Jesus told the woman that her faith had made her well.

3. By allowing the sick to touch his clothes, what does this tell us about Jesus' attitude toward human brokenness? (See Mark 5:24-34 NRSV).

   A. Jesus fully understood that God wants all people to experience wholeness in every dimension of life: spirit, body, mind (emotions), finances, and in our social context. Jesus proved this by demonstrating God's healing power, which was central to his mission and ministry. God sent Jesus to restore His good creation, which encompasses healing, wholeness, and salvation.

4. All the people who touched Jesus' clothes were healed. How does this healing incident challenge your faith to appropriate (take possession of) your healing?

   A. All the people who touched Jesus' clothes were healed because they believed that would be the outcome! This is what is called the appropriating act of faith. Such faith taps into the grace of God. God's grace is open to everyone. We all stand in the streams of God's healing and redemptive grace. A person must not just believe that in the atonement, God's power is available to save sinners; you must also believe that it includes the power that provides healing, wholeness, and deliverance. When you have the peace of Christ and the assurance of God's atoning grace for all your sins, that is the act of appropriating faith. Sadly, we do not carry this act of faith into other life situations, such as healing. The woman claimed her healing through this act of faith. Her faith released the healing power of God that flowed out of Jesus Christ. Another name for appropriating faith is expectant or radical faith!

5. Do you believe that God is with you and cares about your wellbeing as a servant of Christ?

   A. God's redemptive act of allowing His Son to die vicariously for the sins of the world tells me that not only does God care about the wellbeing of humanity, but God also acted to make it possible. He did this by sending humanity a saving and healing Messiah (John 3:16; Isaiah 53; 61 NIV).

6. Could one's faith initiate the creation of a miracle?

   A. The woman who touched the hem of Jesus' clothes initiated her healing miracle. The four men carrying their paralytic friend to Jesus to be healed also helped to initiate his healing. The Leper, who fell at Jesus' feet, begging Jesus to heal him, tapped into the compassion of Jesus to heal him. The list goes on. When human needs are connected with God's love, grace, power, and mercy, miracles happen. It is essential to understand that God's unconditional love for human beings is the purpose of all miracles. God desires our highest good because we are made in God's image and likeness. God does acts of goodness for His name's sake!

7. What motivated the people to bring their sick to be healed by Jesus?

   A. The people were motivated by compassion and love for broken humanity. If we are created in God's image and likeness, such acts of love reflect the Creator.

8. Is there a connection between miracles and the kingdom of God?

   A. When Jesus gave his authority and power to his disciples to heal the sick, cast out demons, and to proclaim the good news of the gospel, the same kingdom work he was doing, this was a revelation to the people that the kingdom of God had broken into human history. To this present time, healing is a visible sign of the present reign of God. Healing is evidence that God's good creation is being restored. Healing is central to God's redemptive, kingdom work.

9. Do you think you have a faith that could appropriate your healing miracles, as did the woman who touched the hem of Jesus' garment?

   A. The healing of this woman reminds us that healing is possible. Healing is in the atonement. Jesus' sacrificial death on the cross atoned for human sin, making forgiveness possible. The prophet Isaiah foretold that God laid our sins and diseases upon Jesus, nailing them to the cross. By his wounds, we are healed (Isaiah 53:4-10). Healing and salvation are the two sides of the same coin. Salvation is ultimate healing!

10. How might the extraordinary miracles God did through Peter's shadow (Acts 5:12-16 NIV) and Paul's handkerchiefs and aprons (Acts 19:11-12 NIV.) help you better understand the healing of the woman who touched the hem of Jesus' garment (Mark 5:24-34 NIV), and the healing of the sick people in the marketplace who touched Jesus' cloak. Explain.

   A. The methods that God uses to heal people should be seen through the lens of God's love. No object, whether Paul's handkerchief and apron, Peter's shadow, or Jesus' cloak, have power within themselves. Each of these objects represents a means of grace that point beyond themselves. They point us to the healing Christ, who represents the healing grace and power of God. These objects were used as a point of contact to help people release their faith in God's healing power.

11. Describe what you will take away from this healing moment that has helped change your perspective on the difference between magic and expectant faith.

   A. Servant ministry is a noble and high calling. It is a privilege to share in the mission and ministry of Jesus Christ, which we should never take for granted. As members of the body of Christ, we are God's agents of change. What we do for God has eternal consequences! Magic is more about fairy tales and has the appearance of religion or even the supernatural, but does not lead us to faith in God. On the other hand, expectant faith depends on the supernatural acts of God's love, power, and grace that provide healing, wholeness, and salvation.

Persistent Healing Faith

Key Concepts

Healing Moment Twelve, "Persistent Healing Faith," challenges us to have persistent and expectant faith in the promises of God. God rewards active, expectant, and persistent faith (Matt. 7:7-11 NRSV). The New Testament discourages unbelief and faithlessness. In the epistle of James, we are told that a person without faith will not receive anything from God (James 1:5-8NRSV). In the book of Hebrews, we read that without faith it is impossible to please God (Heb.11:6 NRSV). This Syrophoenician woman displayed persistent faith.

The news of the fame of Jesus' power to heal the sick and to cast out demons had reached this Hellenistic region, a metropolitan center in the Phoenician republic of Tyre. Hearing of Jesus' extraordinary power over demons and that he was in the region, this mother searched to learn his where abouts. Once she located Jesus' where abouts, she fell at his feet and begged him to go and cast the demon out of her daughter. In her desperation, the woman would not accept no. Through her strong faith, she dismissed Jesus' silence and the disciples desire to get rid of her. She envisioned her daughter delivered from that evil spirit and playing like a normal child.

In her part of the world, many persons were known as miracle workers. Not wanting to be labeled as just a miracle worker, Jesus tested the woman's faith to see if she thought of him in this way. Jesus told the Gentile woman it was not right to take the children's bread and throw it to dogs. The woman did not take Jesus' words as an insult. She let Jesus know she understood divine grace, and that she did not have to deserve grace to receive it. The woman reminded Jesus that even the dogs under the children's tables eat the crumbs that fall to the floor. Jesus was pleased with her faith-filled response and told her to go home that her daughter had been healed. She took Jesus at his word, went home, and found her daughter lying quietly on the bed. The demon was gone.

Jesus was so impressed with her strong, persistent faith that he healed her daughter without praying, touching, or being in the presence of her daughter. Mark's gospel emphasizes over and over that God rewards faith and does not respond to unbelief or faithlessness.

Persistent
Healing Faith

Discovery

1. What was the motive behind Jesus' apparent refusal to heal this
    Gentile woman's daughter?
    A. Jesus was simply being true to his mission to first proclaim the
    good news of the gospel of the kingdom to the Jews. He saw
    this as a teaching moment to introduce this Greek-speaking
    woman to the love and healing grace of God. He wanted to do
    more than to heal her daughter. Jesus wanted her to know that
    in him, God's kingdom reign had broken into human history,
    to both heal and to save.

2. What lesson does this woman teach us about persistent faith and
    resolve? (See Matthew 7:7-11.)
    A. This woman teaches us that God responds to persistent faith.
    Second, she teaches that faith is the catalyst that releases
    God's healing power. Persistent faith does not waver in the
    face of adversity or disappointment.

3. What obstacles did this mother have to overcome to get Jesus to heal her daughter?

    A. This mother of a demon-possessed child had several obstacles to overcome. First, there would be a language barrier. Second, she had to overcome a religious obstacle. Third, the woman had to overcome the rejection of Jesus' disciples and the apparent rejection of Jesus. Fourth, she had to convince Jesus that her faith was genuine in his ability to heal her daughter and that her desperation and grief were justifiable.

4. Was the attitude of Jesus' disciples toward this Gentile woman racially motivated? Explain.

    A. It does not appear so. The disciples simply wanted Jesus to get the necessary rest that he so desperately needed, as well as for themselves. Jesus had gone to a secluded place to rest where he thought he could go unnoticed.

5. Was Jesus' statement, "*for it is not fair to take the children's bread and throw it to the dogs*" (Mark 7:27 NRSV), a put-down of the woman's daughter? Explain.

    A. Jesus' words to this Gentile woman was not designed as a put down of her race or her humanity. His words were to engage her in an honest conversation. By speaking to her as a Jew, she recognized that Jesus was no ordinary Jew. Further, she engaged in conversation with Jesus to let him know that she did not allow the Jews or anyone else, to define who she was in the eyes of God. Furthermore, she convinced Jesus that her faith in his power to heal her daughter was both genuine and urgent.

6. What impressed you most about the way this woman responded to Jesus' objection to heal her daughter?

    A. I was impressed with this woman's persuasive attitude and persistent faith. She knew what she wanted for her daughter, and she knew Jesus was the servant of God that could give her what she wanted. She would not be dissuaded.

7. What lesson will you take away from this healing incident that helps you to respond with dignity and humility toward people of another ethnic group who are in need?

   A. As Christians, we are not to judge or to discount others of another race. We are always to respect the dignity, worth, and value of each person. God calls us to love and to care for each other.

8. Why do you think Jesus felt it necessary to test the faith of this Gentile woman before healing her daughter?

   A. In the Gentile world there were many miracle workers, associated with magic and spiritual influences, which were not of God. Jesus wanted to make sure that his heavenly Father would receive the glory in the healing of her daughter.

9. Does God ever act when faith is absent? Explain.

   A. Yes, God does act when faith is absent. God loves people unconditionally. Most of the times God blesses people for His name's sake. Apostle Paul reminds us that while we were living in sin, God sent His Son, Jesus Christ to die for our sins, a debt none of us could pay. The cross gives evidence that God acts when faith is absent. All of God actions in our lives are motivated by divine love, grace, and mercy.

10. In what situation or circumstance has your persistent faith moved God to answer your prayers?

    A. It is not so much that our faith moves God to respond to our prayers. Our faith moves us to put out trust in God's love and providential care as His people. Because of what Jesus Christ has done for us, we can turn to God to meet all our needs, because He cares for humanity.

11. Describe what you will take away from this Healing Moment that has helped to change your perspective about the relationship between persistent faith and healing?

   A. The relationship between persistent faith and healing seems to have a favorable and positive outcome. God rewards faith, even faith the size of a mustard seed, according to Jesus' teaching on faith.

HEALING MOMENT THIRTEEN

God's Healing Grace Includes Everyone

Key Concepts

Healing Moment Thirteen, "God's Healing Grace Includes Everyone," makes it clear that the gospel of the kingdom of God is universal. God's love embraces all of humanity, which is unconditional. God's love for humanity was powerfully demonstrated by Jesus dying on a cross for the sins of the entire world (John 3:16). It is essential to understand that healing is rooted in love.

Although Jesus Christ was the Jewish Messiah, he was also the Savior of the world. His mission was first to the Jews and through the Jews to spread the gospel of salvation to the entire world. The fact that Gentiles are also being healed is evident that Jesus Christ is the Savior of the world.

The Bible teaches that God is not a respecter of persons and does not show favoritism (Acts 10:34-35; 2 Peter 3:9; 1 Tim. 2:4). Jesus taught his disciples this truth of God also (James 2:9). Jesus and the apostle Paul remind us that for all have sinned and fall short of the glory of God" (Rom. 3:23 NKJV). In Jesus Christ, both Jews and Gentiles alike stand before God on a level playing field, both needing God's healing and saving grace. Jesus' atoning death on the cross is

God's equalizer, the ultimate expression of God's unconditional love. Through his atoning death, Jesus has opened the way for everyone to experience God's healing, wholeness, and salvation.

Mark records three miracles Jesus performed as he ministered in a region of the Gentiles. As Jesus and his disciples traveled from Tyre through Sidon toward the Sea of Galilee, in the region of the Decapolis, he encountered a deaf man with a speech impediment. The man's friends brought him to Jesus, begging him to heal their friend. This healing is unique to Mark's gospel. It is significant because Jesus had just taught the disciples there is no difference between Jews and Gentiles. God loves everyone unconditionally.

Jesus took the man away from the people to heal him in private. He personalized his healing methods to bring about the best results. Because there could be no communication between Jesus and the man, Jesus used touch as a means of communication. He put his finger into the man's ears, then spat and touched the man's tongue. The man received a double blessing of God's healing grace, allowing him to hear perfectly and speak plainly. The people were amazed by this healing miracle. The news of this miracle spread far and wide.

God's Healing Grace Includes Everyone

Discovery

1. Do you believe your physical and spiritual conditions matter to God? Explain why or why not.

   A. Yes! Our spiritual and physical conditions matter to God. All the healing miracles that Jesus performed give evidence to that fact. Jesus heals because he saw his Father healing. Jesus did nothing that his Heavenly Father did not do. Jesus was on a divine mission for his heavenly Father, to bring healing, wholeness, and salvation to broken humanity.

2. What do you suppose Jesus prayed about as he sighed, looking up to heaven?

   A. The New Testament reveals that when Jesus sighed, it was an acknowledgment that the Father always hears His Son's requests to connect human needs with God's power to do good works.

3. What surprised you most about the healing of the deaf and mute man?

    A. The healing of this deaf and mute man is consistent with all the people that Jesus healed. Each healing is personal and creative, emphasizing God's love, compassion, and concern for those who are hurting and suffering.

4. What does the teaching of Jesus teach you about healing that encourages and inspires a desire within you to pray for the sick and suffering?

    A. The healings that Jesus performed remind us how widespread human brokenness and evil exist in the world. It also points out that the healing ministry is both essential and vital in God's kingdom work.

5. What would the church and world look and feel like if the practice of healing were limited only to a particular group of people?

    A. It would show that the gospel of the kingdom was not inclusive, and that God shows favoritism. The Bible teaches that Jesus' mission and ministry in the world have demonstrated that God healing grace is available to everyone.

6. You may not have the gift of healing, but what gifts do you have to share in Jesus' ministry of compassion to people who are suffering?

    A. The church's only gift to bring about healing is *agape* love because healing is rooted in divine love. Having said this, all the *charismata* (grace-gifts) have the potential and creative power to, in some way manifests healing. The Spirit of God has endowed the church with "gifts of healing" to meet every human need for healing (1 Cor. 12:9 NIV).

7. Jesus and his disciples were tired to the bones, yet Jesus reached out to this deaf and mute man. What excuses do you make for not reaching out to those around you who are hurting?

    A. Some Christians believe that God sends sickness to punish sinful people. If so, to whom are we to pray for healing. Others make the excuse that only certain persons have the gift to heal. Still, others believe that healing happened at one time but that all miracles ceased after the apostolic age had passed. Now, that we have hospitals, technology, and medical science, spiritual healing is over-kill. However, none of those excuses are supported by the Scriptures. Furthermore, the resurrected Christ still heals through the church, the body of Christ.

8. In what ways have you allowed the love of money and material things to blind you to the needs of the people around you?
    A. Some people think that money is the panacea that will solve all our problems in this life. The love of money can blind us to our need for salvation. Money can give us a false sense of security. The rich young ruler wrongly thought that his wealth and material goods were all he needed to have a good life, free of trouble and harm (Mark 10:17-27). However, the New Testament teaches us that God is our source and security.

9. How is God calling you to share in Christ's ministry to the hurting and suffering people in your church and community?
    A. It is essential to realize that we are our brothers' and sisters' keepers. Paul tells us to bear one another's burdens (Gal. 6:2). Jesus instructs us to love one another, John 13:34-35). In the gospel of Matthew, Jesus gives the most emphatic teachings on caring for the least of these. Jesus admonishes his followers to care for the vulnerable among us who are: hungry, sick, homeless, naked, and those in prison (See Matt. 25:31-46). Each of these acts of Christian love is expected of everyone who claims to follow Jesus Christ. They remind the poor and needy that God loves and cares about them, which brings both spiritual and physical healing.

10. As you look at the hurting and suffering people in your church community, what gift or gifts do you ask God for in order to minister to those needs?

    A. The apostle Paul reminds us that no matter what spiritual gifts we possess if we do not have love, our gifts are worthless and useless because love is essential for their operation. Paul places love above the *charismata* in importance. He lists three spiritual things that last forever: faith, hope, and love. Of these three things, love is the greatest of them. Therefore, we should ask for the gift of love to serve others.

11. Describe what you will take away from this healing moment that has helped change your perspective on the difference between magic and expectant faith.

    A. The writer of the book of Hebrews tells us that "...*without faith, it is impossible to please God*" (Heb. 11:6-12 NIV). God rewards faith but rejects magic. Why? Faith demonstrates our dependence on God, whereas magic shows our reliance on ourselves.

A Miracle That Required Two Attempts

Key Concepts

Healing Moment Fourteen, "A Miracle That Required Two Attempts," demonstrates the negative spiritual impact concerning unbelief, including healing. Mark reveals that Jesus could only heal a few folks in Bethsaida because of the lack of faith among the people. This healing story is connected to the healing of a deaf man in Mark 7:31 37. In both stories, people bring them to Jesus that he might touch and heal them. In both stories, Jesus takes the deaf men away from the people, touching and healing them. These healing stories are unique to Mark's Gospel. Mark alone lists three healing miracles where Jesus performs in secret because of unbelief. Jesus removed the scornful, unbelieving group of professional mourners when he heals Jairus's daughter (Mark 5:35-43).1 Because Jesus discerned a strong sense of unbelief among the people in their villages, he healed the two blind and mute men outside of their villages, away from the unbelieving people (Mark 7:33; 8:23). Both blind men had once been sighted persons.

His discernment seemed to be confirmed because he had difficulty healing the blind man. When Jesus laid his hand on the blind man, he was only partially healed. His vision was still blurred, and he could not see at a distance. He saw men looking like trees. This was the first time Jesus questioned his efforts to heal anyone. Because of the blind man's partial healing, he laid his hand on his eyes a second time. This time, the man could see correctly.

In each of these healing stories, Jesus warns the healed men not to return to their village. The prophet speaks of those kinds of miracles that will accompany God's final salvation. Each of the healing stories has similarities in wording, and Mark seems to suggest an essential connection to Isaiah 35:5-6, because Isaiah speaks of the person being spiritually blind and deaf. Mark's reference to the healing of persons deaf and blind suggests that such miracles identify Jesus as God's servant, who will come as the healing Messiah of Israel. As the Messiah of God, Jesus will open the eyes of those spiritually blind to the salvation of God. The Messiah will also open the eyes of the physically blind, demonstrating his power over Satan, who causes both forms of blindness.

The healing of the deaf and mute men makes it clear that God rewards faith. Unbelief is often an obstacle to healing or receiving anything from God. We also learn that no healing is beyond Jesus' ability to heal, whether there is a lack of faith or not. Jesus makes the point that faith is always a factor in the healing process. Both healing stories reveal that Jesus is never too tired or too busy to help those in need of God's grace and healing power.

A Miracle That Required Two Attempts

Discovery

1. What made the healing of the blind man an unusual healing event?
    A. The healing of this blind man or any other person was the first time Jesus had to pray for a second time before the healing was completed.

2. How do the healings of the deaf man in Mark 7:31-37 and the blind man in Mark 8:22-26, seem both weird and wonderful at the same time?
    A. The healing of each of these men was weird because Jesus had to take them away from the unbelieving people before he could heal them. Jesus used his own spit and human touch to heal the men. Each of these healing miracles brought honor and glory to God and amazement to the people, because they had never seen God's power demonstrated in this way.

3. Did Mark intend to make a connection between the apparent spiritual blindness of the disciples, and the two men healed by Jesus of their blindness? (See Mark 8:22-26; 10: 46-52.)

    A. Mark wanted the disciples and his readers to understand that there was an apparent connection between their spiritual blindness and the physical blindness of the men Jesus had healed. Their spiritual blindness had prevented them from recognizing Jesus as their Messiah by the many miracles God demonstrated through him. The miracles of healing the sick, casting out demons, having power over nature, and raising the dead proved that he was their long-awaited Messiah.

4. List several things that make this healing story different from all the others Jesus performed (Mark 8:22-26).

    A. First, these healings demonstrate God's personal concern about each human being. Not only is healing personal, but it also reveals God's fatherly compassion for humanity.

5. Is there evidence that this man was not born blind?

    A. It was apparent that the man had once been able to see, because he was able to describe how both a man and a tree looked.

6. Considering that Jesus had to lay his hands on the blind man's eyes a second time before he was completely healed, what should the church learn from this healing story?

    A. There is much mystery in healing. The church should learn that healing is central to the kingdom work of God. Second, God has gifted and empowered the church to continue Christ's threefold ministry of teaching, preaching, and healing until his return. Third, the church is Christ's representatives in both the church and world as his hands, feet, and voice.

7. Although the healing of the blind man was a two-step and gradual process, can it still be considered a miracle?

    A. A miracle may happen instantly or gradually as was in the case of the two-step process of healing the blind man.

8. Why do you think Jesus isolated himself from the people in the healing of this blind man?

    A. Let us not forget that Jesus healed the blind man in spite of the unbelieving village people. This is why he led the man outside of the village. His isolation of himself from the people was an indictment of their lack of faith in the love, goodness, mercy, power, and healing grace of God.

9. The four gospels recorded Jesus' healing at least seven persons who were blind. List the different methods he used to heal each of them.

    A. Each of the methods Jesus' used to heal the blind men reveal God's intimate knowledge of the individual needs of each person who turns to Him for healing. Healing is both individualized and holistic.

10. Why do you think Jesus used different methods to heal the blind and the people in general?

    A. The answer given above may be applied here, also.

HEALING MOMENT FIFTEEN

Prayer, Not Human Power Overcomes Demons

Key Concepts

Healing Moment Fifteen, "Prayer, Not Human Power, Overcomes Demons," is brought to the forefront in this healing incident and is also revealed throughout the New Testament. The primary focus of Jesus' messianic mission was to defeat the evil and demonic work of Satan. His healing ministry included setting people free from demonic oppression. Mark makes it clear that those who have put their faith and trust in God through Christ have been given the same power and authority to resist and defeat Satan's evil forces (Mark 3:15; 6:12-13; Matt. 10:1-2; Luke 9:12; 10:17-20).

A father brought his sick son to Jesus who was being tormented by an evil spirit, in hopes that Jesus would cast out the demon. However, the father did not know that Jesus was not in the area at that time. The desperate father asked the disciples to cast out the evil spirit. They were not able to cast out the spirit. When Jesus, Peter, James, and John came down from the mountain, a large crowd of people were arguing with the disciples. Jesus asked the people about what they were arguing. The father explained that he had asked his disciples to cast out the evil spirit from his son. When Jesus learned that the disciples could not cast out the spirit, Jesus expressed his strong disappointment with them.

The casting out of demons was not something that was new to his disciples. Previously, they had healed many and cast out many demons (Mark 6:12-13). Jesus wanted to know why this was a problem for them with this boy. Jesus questioned the faith of his disciples and was disturbed by it all. Jesus had the father to bring his son to him. When the demon saw Jesus, it immediately threw the child into a convulsion, causing him to fall to the ground. Jesus asked the father how long his son had been in this condition? The father said, "From childhood."

This healing incident reminds us that followers of Jesus Christ have been given the power and authority to cast out evil spirits (demons), which the New Testament strongly supports. Jesus anticipated that his disciples would continue his threefold ministry of teaching, preaching, and healing. Jesus later told his disciples that having a strong prayer life was essential to exercising the power and authority of God to overcome demon spirits.

As I bring out in the book, *Miracles of Healing in the Gospel of Mark*, Jesus has given God's power and authority to the church to overcome the works of Satan. This same power frees us to love God and neighbor, and the carrying out of the Great Commission. The Bible calls this the Spirit-filled life. The Holy Spirit makes the resurrected Christ's presence real to the church. When the church moves in love, unity, and purpose, there is no power on earth that the church, the body of Christ cannot defeat, including Satan and his demons.

Prayer, Not Human Power Overcomes Demons

Discovery

1. What caused Jesus to be so exasperated with his disciples concerning this healing incident?

   A. Jesus was exasperated with his disciples because they were trying to cast out the evil spirit in their own human strength and power. Human ingenuity is no match against demonic power and evil. Jesus pointed out the primary reason for their failure to heal the boy was an impoverished prayer life.

2. The disciples had successfully cast out demons previously. Why were they unable to cast out this unclean spirit from this man?

   A. Questions one and two may seem like the same question. However, it is essential to understand that in ministry, we represent Christ. As Christian believers, we represent Christ Jesus' presence, power, and authority. Demons are quick to size-up believers. They can discern the strengths and weaknesses of their opponents. Demons can discern those believers that spend quality time in prayer with God.

They can sense a person that abides in Christ and in his word (John 15:1-8; Acts 19:15-17). Jesus also emphasizes that human power is never a substitute for prayer in ministry. Jesus reveals that dealing with certain evil spirits requires both faith and prayer. Matthew records Jesus' words as to why prayer is so essential in the life of the Christian. When Jesus asked his disciples to pray in the garden of Gethsemane, he meant this more for their strengthening than for him. Seeing that they were having a challenging time staying awake and praying, Jesus gives Peter, this warning. *"Watch and pray so that you will not fall into temptation. The spirit is willing, but the flesh is weak"* (Mark 14:38 NIV). Prayer sharpens our sensitivity to God's prompting and guidance and strengthens us spiritually to avoid the temptations of Satan. Prayer helps us to shore-up our reliance on God and not in our human strength, ability, or power.

3. Did the disciples' inability to cast out the demon from the boy shake the father's confidence in Jesus' ability to heal his son?

   A. Not at all. After the father witnessed the disciples' inability to heal his son, this may have weakened his faith in Jesus' ability to cast the evil spirit out of his son. However, he quickly confirmed his faith in Jesus to heal his son. The man tells Jesus, *"I do believe; help me overcome my unbelief"* (Mark 9:24 NIV)! Jesus' response to the father should reveal to all believers the power and authority of Jesus supremacy over demons: *"Everything is possible for him who believes"* (v. 23). Jesus rebuked the evil spirit: *You deaf and mute spirit...I command you, come out of him and never enter him again"* (Mark 9:25b NIV).

4. Are you letting God use the gifts He has given you to liberate your brothers and sisters from the work of evil spirits? If so, in what ways?

    A. From my experience, exorcism or casting out demons has not been something that many Christians have experienced, particular in the mainline denominations. However, for those who participate in this unique study, hopefully, this will change. People will realize that exorcism is central to the practice of healing in the kingdom work of God. Mark stresses that the conflict between Satan and God is ongoing. The church must step up and take her rightful place to continue Christ's mission and ministry to confront and defeat evil and suffering, until his return.

5. Why is prayer necessary in casting our evil spirits?

    A. Jesus taught and modeled the importance of prayer. Prayer to God in Jesus' name demonstrated that to those confronting evil spirits, that it is God's power that is being relied upon and not the human flesh. When God's people make prayer central to everything we say and do, demons will have to heed and obey. (See Luke 10:17-20 NIV.)

6. Is there ever a time when human power is a substitute for prayer in casting out an evil spirit? Explain.

    A. Human power is never a substitute for prayer. According to Jesus, prayer is essential keep us from relying on the human flesh and to help us avoid the subtleness and deception of Satan, which leads people into temptation. Prayer is the greatest spiritual weapon of the church. Prayer is faith in action. Prayer and faith are the catalyst for miracles.

7. Describe a situation when you failed to accomplish a spiritual task because you had not spent quality time with God in prayer. What lesson did you learn from that experience?

   A. Most Christians struggle with not spending quality time with God. As a result of this, many Christians are weak and ineffective in their relationship and walk with God.

8. List several ways prayer affects one's faith.

   A. Prayer and faith are two of the spiritual pillars of the Christian faith. Prayer demonstrates our reliance on God for our effectiveness in servant ministry.

9. How did the verbal exchange between Jesus and the father strengthen the father's faith?

   A. Clearly, Jesus met the father where he was spiritually, but challenged him to recognize his lack of faith. The exchange between them, moved the father to put all his faith and trust in God's power to work through Jesus to heal his son. When the father heard Jesus say: *"Everything is possible for him who believes"* (Mk. 9:22 NIV), this moved and strengthened the father's faith in Jesus' ability to heal his son.

10. Previously, the disciples had cast out demons. (See Mark 6:13.) What do Matthew and Luke give as the reason the disciples were unable to cast out the evil spirit in the boy? (See Matt. 17:14-19; Luke 9:37-45.)

    A. Both Matthew and Luke agreed with Mark that the disciples' lack of prayer and faith, weakened their ability to demonstrate God's power and authority to liberate this boy from the evil spirit. Jesus was extremely upset with them because this would give the people a false impression that Satan's power was greater than that of God and of himself. Mark pointed out that the spiritual weakness and faithlessness of Jesus' disciples were both unreasonable and intolerable. Jesus had shown over and over that he reigned supreme over demons. He had also transferred God's power and authority to his disciples to cast out demons. Like Jesus, the disciples had demonstrated their faith to exorcise many demons. For their failure to heal this boy, Jesus referred to them as a faithless and perverse generation, calling into question God's power and authority.

11. Read the following passages of scripture: Mark 1:23-27; 5:1-20; 9:14-29. What patterns of demon activity did Mark want his readers to pay attention to?

A. Interestingly, most of the demonic activity occurred in a synagogue. Think about how much demonic activity might also be happening in the church. Someone has said that the church is a spiritual hospital. For this reason, the church must take healing more seriously as a viable and essential ministry. The demons identified the two natures of Jesus. They traumatized both their victims and the community or region. Mark also revealed that much of human suffering is demon related. Mark showed that demon activity is universal in scope. Finally, the conflict between Satan and God is systemic and ongoing, but Satan will come to a destructive end when Jesus returns, to establish God's kingdom on earth. (See Mark 1:23-26; Luke 4:33-35.)

HEALING MOMENT SIXTEEN

Your Faith Has Made You Well

Key Concepts

The final Healing Moment is "Your Faith Has Made You Well." The healing of blind Bartimaeus is the last healing miracle recorded in Mark's Gospel. The healing of Bartimaeus is unique to Mark. First, it is unique because Bartimaeus was the first person, Jesus healed that was named by Mark. Second, it is noteworthy for being the only healing miracle of a blind person that Jesus neither touched nor prayed for. He declared, *"Go, your faith has made you well" (Mark 10:52a NRSV)*. In the Old Testament, blindness was considered a curse (John 9:1-10). Mark shows that it was this blind man who identified Jesus in the lineage of King David, as the Messiah of Israel. "He opens the eyes of the blind." The one who opens the eyes of the blind, would soon give his life on a cross, who redeemed us from the curse of the law (Gal. 3:13 NIV).

Third, Mark emphasized the importance of personal faith in the healing process. According to Mark, faith is the catalyst that releases God's power to heal. Mark affirmed that God rewards expectant and persistent faith.

Bartimaeus had that kind of faith. God does not validate unbelief or doubt. James affirmed this spiritual principle (James 1:6-8). Fourth, Mark stressed over and over that human wholeness or wellbeing is central in the mind and will of God for human beings.

The healing of Bartimaeus was a defining moment in the mission of Jesus, concluding his Galilean ministry. Jesus' attention was now focused on Jerusalem and the cross. As he and his disciples were leaving Jericho, he encountered a beggar named Bartimaeus, sitting by the roadside begging for money. Hearing the commotion of the people traveling through the area, the blind man asked what was going on. Someone from the crowd told him that Jesus was passing by. Bartimaeus cried out, *"Son of David, have mercy on me!"* Many in the crowd tried to silence him, but the more they tried, the more he cried out to Jesus. His cries stopped Jesus in his tracks, and he told the people to call the man to him.

Bartimaeus immediately threw off his outer garment and made his way to Jesus. Jesus asked him, *"What do you want me to do for you"* (Mark 10:51 NRSV)? Bartimaeus replied, *"My teacher, let me see again."* Without touching him or saying a prayer for his healing, Jesus commended him for his faith and said, *"Go, your faith has made you well"* (Mark 10:52 NRSV). Immediately, he regained his sight and followed Jesus on the way.

What is extraordinary about Bartimaeus's healing is that there seems to be an air of expectancy and excitement in Jesus. Perhaps hearing Bartimaeus calling him by his messianic title, Son of David (used only in the synoptic gospels), may have caused Jesus to reflect on his mission as the savior of his Jewish people and the world. This title was used to refer to Jesus as the Messiah. Jesus made many claims that he is the messianic hope of Israel.

Even though the ordeal of the cross loomed in Jesus' immediate future, he took the time to heal a blind man sitting by the road. This healing was a significant transition in Jesus' life and ministry, and would be such in the life of his disciples. His earthly kingdom work was coming to its divine end, while the disciples' ministry was about to begin. Jesus' focus now shifts to Jerusalem and the cross. He went to the Jewish feast to embrace his messianic vocation.[1] This was an indication that his mission was on the right course. The road leading to the cross opened a path to God's redemption work to bring salvation to Israel and the world.

Your Faith Has Made You Well

Discovery

1. Why was it necessary for Jesus to go to Jerusalem? What did that have to do with his messianic mission?

    A. Jesus' earthly mission was coming to its divine fulfillment. Jesus' focus was now on Jerusalem and the cross. He was destined to go to Jerusalem, not only because the Jewish Passover celebration was at hand, that the time had come for him as the eternal lamb of God to give his life as a ransom for the sins of the world,

2. Could Bartimaeus's throwing off his cloak suggests that he envisioned the recovery of his sight?

    A. Throwing off his cloak, suggests that he believed that Jesus would be God's instrument to show him divine mercy and grace in restoring his sight. Leaving his cloak behind as a make-shift bed indicated that he would no longer need it with his eyesight restored.

3. Read second Samuel 7:14-17 and Psalm 89:3-4. What connection is Mark attempting to make between King David, Jesus, and Jerusalem? (See also Isaiah 11:1f; Jeremiah 23:5f; Ezekiel 34:23.)

   A. It seems reasonable that Bartimaeus had heard of the many miracles that God had demonstrated through Jesus. When he heard that it was Jesus of Nazareth passing through, he was excited and cried out to Jesus, the Son of David, to have mercy on him. Mark wanted to show his readers that Jesus was God's divine fulfillment of restoring the blessings and mercies to Israel. Mark used the physical healing of blind Bartimaeus as a prelude to removing the spiritual blindness of the Israelites and his disciples. He makes this healing central to the context of Bartimaeus' reference to Jesus, as the Son of David, a Messianic title. Mark shows the connection between Jesus, David, and Jerusalem, which is the city of David. The purpose of this healing miracle was to challenge his readers to recognize their spiritual blindness, and cry out to Jesus, as Bartimaeus had done, to heal and remove their blindness. When God would cure their blindness, their perspective of Jesus would be radically changed. Then, they would be able to see their long-awaited Messiah in the person of Jesus Christ. Jesus Christ was God's Suffering Servant who had come to heal and save the Hebrew people and the world.

4. Why do you think Mark only gave the name of this blind beggar and none of the other individuals healed by Jesus?

   A. The naming of blind Bartimaeus is recorded only in the gospel of Mark. Bartimaeus means "son of Timaeus." The gospels' writers usually associated the name of an individual that is important to some event or story that is central to the narrative of the gospel or revelation of Jesus' mission and ministry.

5. Is it possible that Mark recorded these healing stories to reveal to his readers that Jesus is in fact, the Son of God—the Messiah of Israel?

   A. Most likely, Mark recorded these healing stories as a way of introducing to his readers that Jesus was the Messiah of Israel.

6. Read Isaiah 29:18; 35:5- 6; 53:4-10; 61. How do these scriptures define Jesus' redemptive mission as the son of God?

   A. Each of the miracles reveals a significant aspect of Jesus' mission and ministry as the Messianic Suffering Servant of God. He will cause the blind to see, the deaf to hear, the good news preached to the poor, and cause the lame to walk. Jesus is the anointed Messiah of God sent to heal and redeem Israel and the world.

7. Why was Bartimaeus's healing, which took place outside of Jericho, so crucial to Jesus' overall ministry?

   A. Jericho was a city twenty miles northeast of Jerusalem. The healing of Bartimaeus was the final healing miracle that Jesus performed on his way to Jerusalem to lay down his life as a ransom for the sins of humanity, that no one but he could pay. Mark used the healing of a blind man named Bartimaeus as a prelude to when the Israelites' spiritual blindness would be removed that had blinded them from recognizing Jesus as their Messiah. Ironically, this blind man was able to see with his heart that Jesus was the long-awaited Messiah. Yet even those with good or perfect vision were blind to Jesus' being their Messiah. Healing the blind both physically and spiritually would be one of the miraculous signs of that accompany the Messiah of God.

8. Do you know someone who has received his or her site through prayer or medical intervention?

   A. Yes! A young boy about fourteen years old was healed when I laid my hand on him. He was born with an eye disease that left him with no depth perception. He was healed instantly, but he did not know it at the time. Later, the healing of his eyes would be confirmed by his eye doctor.

9. How did Bartimaeus's life change after he received his restored vision?

   A. Interestingly, Jesus did not only open the eyes of blind Bartimaeus, but he also opened the spiritual eyes of his heart and gained a new disciple and member of the kingdom of God. With his new sight and a transformed heart, Bartimaeus followed Jesus on his way to Jerusalem, where he may have witnessed Jesus' sacrificial death on a cross.

10. Is there some form of blindness in you that Jesus needs to heal?

    A. We all require some kind of healing, whether physical, spiritual, emotional, or relational. Knowing this, we can trust God for our healing through Jesus Christ.

ABOUT THE AUTHOR

Dr. John I. Penn is a retired ordained United Methodist minister. From 2002 to 2008, Dr. Penn served as the pastor of Simpson United Methodist Church in Wilmington, Delaware. Before coming to Simpson, Penn served seven-and-a-half years as the Director of Spiritual Formation and Healing at Upper Room Ministries in Nashville, Tennessee. As an ordained minister, he has served several pastorates in the Peninsula-Delaware Annual Conference. He has served the church for thirty-five years. Penn has served in two cross-racial appointments as an associate pastor.

Penn is a native of Roanoke, Virginia. He is the author of several books: *Rediscovering Our Spiritual Gifts* (Upper Room Books), a companion workbook for Dr. Charles Bryant's book of the same title; *Getting Well, A Study for Children about Spiritual and Physical Healing* (originally published by Abingdon Press); *Equipped to Serve, A Study for Children about the Gifts of the Holy Spirit; About Caring and Healing, An Activities and Coloring Book for Children;* and *Turning Mourning into Dancing, an Adult Coloring Book.* Penn wrote this unique resource as a way to help him move through the grieving process of the death of his mother. She transitioned to be with the Lord on April 14, 2017.

He has also written booklets for youth and children: *What Everyone Should Know about Healing* (Companion to *About Caring and Healing*); *Understanding the Gifts of the Holy Spirit;* and *About the Gifts of the Holy Spirit.*

Penn holds degrees from the University of Arkansas at Pine Bluff (Bachelor of Science in Music Education), Oral Roberts University (Master of Theology), Eastern Baptist Theological Seminary [now Palmer Theological Seminary] (Master of Divinity), and Wesley Theological Seminary (Doctor of Ministry).

He enjoys playing tennis, writing, composing music, reading, gardening, and listening to jazz. He is married to Gloria J. Parker Penn, the author of *Miracles Still Happen.* They have been blessed with six children (one deceased), ten grandchildren, and three great-grandchildren.

SELECTED BIBLIOGRAPHY

Barclay, William. *The Gospel of Mark*. Philadelphia: The Westminster Press, 1975.

Basham, Don. *Deliver Us from Evil*. Grand Rapids: Chosen Books, 1972, 2005.

Hurtado, Larry W. *New International Biblical Commentary*. Massachusetts: *Hendrickson Publisher*, 1983, 1989.

Kelsey, Morton. *Healing and Christianity*. San Francisco: Harper and Row, 1995.

Kingsbury, J. D. *The Christology of Mark's Gospel*. Philadelphia: Fortress, 1983.

Lane, William. L. *The Gospel of Mark: The New International Commentary on the New Testament*. Grand Rapids: Eerdmans, 1974.

MacArthur, John. *The MacArthur Bible Commentary*. Nashville: Thomas Nelson, 2005.

MacNutt, Francis. *Deliverance from Evil Spirits*. Grand Rapids: Chosen Books, 1995, 2009.

Wiersbe, Warren W. *Be Diligent, NT Mark*. Colorado Spring: David C. Cook, 1987.

ENDNOTES

1   Penn, John I. *Rediscovering Our Spiritual Gifts*. Nashville: Upper Rooms Books (1996), 8-9.

Healing Moment One: The Healing Power of Jesus' Words

1   Hurtado, Larry W. *New International Biblical Commentary*. Massachusetts: Hendrickson Publisher (1983, 1989), 27.
2   Kingsbury, Jack Dean. *The Christology of Mark's Gospel*. Philadelphia: Fortress Press, (1893), 83-84.
3   Ibid., 83.
4   Lane, William L. *The Gospel of Mark*. The New International Commentary on the New Testament. Grand Rapids: Eerdmans (1974), 74-75.
5   Ibid., 100.

Healing Moment Two: God's Amazing Healing Grace

1   Wiersbe, Warren W. *Be Diligent, NT Mark*. Colorado Spring: David C. Cook, (1987), 24.

Healing Moment Five: Healing is Always Lawful

1   MacArthur, John. *The MacArthur Bible Commentary*. Nashville: Thomas Nelson (2005), 1203.

Healing Moment Thirteen: God's Healing Grace Includes Everyone

1   Lane, William L. *The Gospel of Mark*. The New International Commentary on the New Testament. Grand Rapids: Eerdmans (1974), 266.

Healing Moment Fourteen: A Miracle that Required Two Attempts

1   Pickett, Wilson. "Nine-Nine and One-Half Won't Do."
2   Hurtado, 133.

Healing Moment Sixteen: Your Faith Has Made You Well

1   Lane, 387; Psalm 42:4.

Printed in the United States
by Baker & Taylor Publisher Services